**W9-BCQ-744**

Best Easy Bike Rides
Minneapolis and Saint Paul

## Help Us Keep This Guide Up to Date

Every effort has been made by the author and editors to make this guide as accurate and useful as possible. However, many things can change after a guide is published—trails are rerouted, regulations change, techniques evolve, facilities come under new management, etc.

We appreciate hearing from you concerning your experiences with this guide and how you feel it could be improved and kept up to date. While we may not be able to respond to all comments and suggestions, we'll take them to heart and we'll also make certain to share them with the author. Please send your comments and suggestions to the following address

> FalconGuides
> Reader Response/Editorial Department
> 246 Goose Lane
> Guilford, CT 06437

Or you may e-mail us at:
> editorial@falcon.com.

Thanks for your input, and happy cycling!

Best Easy Bike Rides Series

# Best Easy Bike Rides Minneapolis and Saint Paul

## Steve Johnson

**FALCON**GUIDES

GUILFORD, CONNECTICUT

# FALCONGUIDES®

An imprint of The Rowman & Littlefield Publishing Group, Inc.
4501 Forbes Blvd., Ste. 200
Lanham, MD 20706
www.rowman.com
Falcon and FalconGuides are registered trademarks and Make Adventure Your Story is a trademark of The Rowman & Littlefield Publishing Group, Inc.

Distributed by NATIONAL BOOK NETWORK

British Library Cataloguing-in-Publication Information available

Library of Congress Control Number: 2019043558
ISBN 978-1-4930-5194-6 (paperback)
ISBN 978-1-4930-5195-3 (e-book)

♾™ The paper used in this publication meets the minimum requirements of American National Standard for Information Sciences—Permanence of Paper for Printed Library Materials, ANSI/NISO Z39.48-1992.

The author and The Rowman & Littlefield Publishing Group, Inc., assume no liability for accidents happening to, or injuries sustained by, readers who engage in the activities described in this book.

# Contents

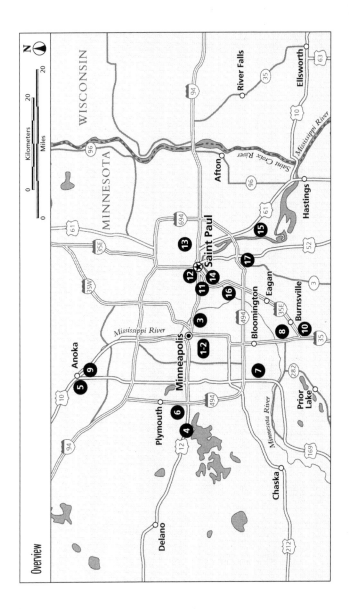

Overview

# Preface

*A good life is when you smile often, dream big, laugh a lot, and realize how blessed you are for what you have.*

—*Anonymous*

A keen observation, and my bet is it was uttered by someone on a bike. I was about 10, smiling and about to realize a dream, when Dad helped me build a little BMX/cruiser Frankenstein bike, cobbled together with cast-off (or pilfered) parts from by brother's bike, rusty nuts and washers, and anything else within reach. Rolling down our cracked and faded driveway for the first time on my new rig, with a black paint job that looked just like the grizzled pavement, I couldn't muster an elegant quote like Anonymous did, but my hoots and hollers of delight felt just as poignant.

Like most squirrely, outdoor-loving kids, I saw summer, and every other season, from the seat of my bike, noodling along the gravel roads and deer trails and field paths around my country neighborhood and small hometown. Those two wheels were an outlet for pent-up energy and a vehicle for adventure. Could we make it all the way to town for a candy bar? How far down the hill can we skid the rear tire?

With longer legs and a 10-speed in the summer before high school, Dad lashed a beat-up tent and ragged sleeping bags to our bikes, and we rode in cutoffs and T-shirts way over our fitness levels on a two-day odyssey to our Wisconsin cabin. Years later in Southern California, my buddy Doug, winning races without ever training, sparked a competitive streak, and I dabbled in racing for a while. A progression of just riding around to touring to hitting the afterburners has me back where I started, savoring the journey and getting out there.

One thing I do have in common with Anonymous is being blessed with what I have, and after the important stuff—roof over my head, great kids, food on the table—I live in a killer place to ride a bike. The Twin Cities are overlaid with a spaghetti tangle of cycling routes, following velvet-smooth pathways along intimate creeks, vibrant city neighborhoods, wide boulevards, and quiet country roads. You can spin a leisurely loop overlooking the Mississippi River, with a patio lunch stop, or hammer 80 hilly, quad-crushing miles. All the action is supported by a hyper-dedicated and enthusiastic core of pedal power fans running the gamut from tykes on trikes to hipster and spit-polished bike shops, pro racers, high-profile government brass and grassroots coalitions, and easygoing cruisers. Heading to the office by bike has become so popular, every Minneapolis office building is required to have bicycle storage, and every city bus and train is equipped to carry bikes. Winters of late have not stemmed the tide, either. There has always been a diehard faction of riders who never tire of layering up wide as the Michelin Man to keep pedaling, but the draw now is stronger than ever. The mild (embarrassing, really, for natives) winters surely have stoked this fire, but there is an almost palpable feel out there that people are amped to be on their bikes all year, even when the city is frozen. Join the fun and ride with like-minded friends in a local bike club. The metro area is packed with great clubs, from recreational to full-on racing. Check out groups like the Twin Cities Bicycling Club, the largest in town, with a year-round calendar of spectacular rides all over the place for all abilities. It's always more fun to log some miles with a buddy.

Where to ride might be as easy as rolling out the back door for some, but even hometown residents don't know every mile in every neighborhood, and a new twist on old favorites is good for the soul. This book features seventeen rides in and around the Twin Cities, selected to present an array of choices for the many moods and desires and skill levels of area riders. I've ridden here all my life and chose routes I deemed worthy of our state's two-wheeled fanatics, including many of my personal go-to rides. I'm continually amazed at the quality and variety of miles available to us here, and how it just keeps getting better. There are bike lanes appearing on more roadways, new bike paths being constructed or old ones repaved, and there always seems to be a new mountain bike trail built or extended or beefed up. Best thing is, there are more people riding than I've ever seen. The other day I saw a family of six merrily riding along a path; they crossed the road in front of me, strung across the entire intersection like a gaggle of ducklings following their parents. Dad in front with the dog, mom pulling a toddler in a bike trailer, and two adorable girls behind on bikes with streamers on their handlebars. Hope, and an unforgettable day with the kids, springs eternal from the seat of a bike.

There is not nearly enough space in this, or any, book to include all of the great ride destinations in the Cities, and it is a tall order to write a best-of book that appeases everyone. Calling theses rides the "best" is, of course, a matter of opinion. I get to do it by having my name on the cover, but your best ride might not be here, your local bike shop probably has a route they love, and some of you might think a few of these just don't warrant a "best" title. It's a select group, to be sure; I gathered intel on a sampling of what I believe shows off our towns' finest riding locales, and I hope you will enjoy the picks. Caveat: I did my best on these pages to present the ride details along with entertaining, or at least informative, text. To accomplish that I had to be more than just a writer. I also wore the hats of cartographer, historian, investigator, photographer, and ambassador. Please forgive any flubs, and toast the successes.

My sincere gratitude to all the bike shop managers I pestered; Gary Sjoquist from Quality Bicycle Products for his otherworldly dedication to our sport; Ryan Lieske and all of the volunteers with MORC; Rich Omdahl and Sue Seeger for the inspirational Hillside trails; Loren Stiles for making me stronger; Nick Pettis, Chris Nelson, and Wayne Hoklas for generous assistance in the field; Rachael Wood; Kimberly Streich; and the entire team at Falcon.

I hope you will enjoy reading and using this book as much as I had writing it. I'm glad I had the opportunity to share my experiences and favorite routes with you. Grab your bike and go for a ride. Hope to see you out there!

# Introduction

The best in the country.

Always finishing with the front-runners, Minneapolis gained two-wheeled supremacy in 2010 as the nation's #1 bike city in *Bicycling* magazine's annual ranking, nudging aside Portland, longtime ruler of this throne. A cyclist from, say, Boulder, might smugly wonder how our short-seasoned, terminally cold town earned such lofty laurels. Ask any rider on our hometown streets and he or she will say, yeah, of course this is the best city, and what took so long? We don't have skyscraping mountains, crashing ocean surf, or palm-lined boulevards, but we have lakes—lots of them—and thousands of miles of rivers, like nowhere else, near which we recreate with verve all year long. Our metro area celebrates water with pathways and pavilions and open space filled with trails and teeming with wildlife, and we gravitate to them like little kids to a sledding hill. Minnesota's outdoor heritage is rich with explorers and historical sports firsts, such as intrepid voyageurs paddling untold miles of wilderness, the invention of waterskiing, and early ski jumping champions. Self-propelled fans carry that tradition proudly today, packing our parks and trails, roads and waterways to simply get out there in this special place or to push themselves to new competitive limits. Industry followed to meet our demands for the best gear, particularly in the bicycle world, with titans like Park Tool, HED Cycling, and Quality Bicycle Products all based right here, innovating, promoting, and supplying the world with all the right stuff.

Another of our big wins is Nice Ride Minnesota, a nonprofit bike-share program launched in 2010 through the Twin Cities Bike Share Project initiative and the City of Lakes Nordic Ski Foundation (more details in the "Area Clubs and Advocacy Groups" section). Surrounding suburbs are also staying vigilant of their residents' two-wheeled wishes, with comprehensive cycling programs and blankets of bike routes over their streets, all working to keep the Twin Cities at the top of the best-of list.

And at the top we will stay, because on any given day there is a kid on a bike with a gleam in his or her eye, pedaling behind Dad on a Saturday morning to the bakery next to the neighborhood bike shop, where a group of elite racers roll out for a training ride, passing a grinning man in his 80s spinning slowly on an old Schwinn to fetch the morning paper and a cup of coffee. Yeah, it really is about the bike, and here in the Twin Cities, the bike is life.

## About the Twin Cities

Minneapolis and Saint Paul are indeed twins in that they are geographically side by side and share a common bond in the Mississippi River, but they have distinctly different personalities. Minneapolis has been likened to a West Coast city, with its urban artsy chic, action-packed nightlife, and glimmering office towers. The city's park system is legendary and a very visible and key cog in its character, as seen most every summer day in the healthy and active vibe around Lakes Calhoun and Harriet. Saint Paul is more relaxed, cradled by bluffs and elegant, European-inspired historic districts, with an oft-quieter mood. Stately boulevards give way to miles of forested river frontage blending into a picturesque river harbor. In cycling-speak, Minneapolis is kind of like a track bike, full speed with no brakes, while Saint Paul is a balloon-tire cruiser. Both cities do, however, combine their characters to make this an award-winning place to call home.

Each downtown boasts a vibrant arts scene, with renowned theaters and museums and a stacked schedule of headliner performances. An array of Fortune 500 corporations base their operations here, and amateur and pro sports teams perform on grand stages like Target Field and the Xcel Energy Center. Both have qualities of the other, being such close siblings and all, like miles and miles of book-worthy riding; a yearlong calendar of lively, two-wheeled events; and a cycling community forged from the very essence of the sport.

On the ground, the Twin Cities reflect the same glacially influenced origin as the rest of the state, highlighted by lakes and rivers and gently rolling topography. You won't find Alps-like climbing here, but there are enough short, steep hills to test your legs, especially in and around the river bluffs; the mix of flat, riverside cruising in town and undulating countryside in surrounding communities rounds out a palette of made-to-order riding terrain.

The latitude line on the globe makes the Twin Cities the coldest major metro area in the United States. Bah! Think a little snow and cold slows us down? Sure, climate-controlled skyways were inspired here so people could move about the cities with normal body temperature, and it's often cold enough outside to freeze off a finger, but that's what we're made of and what makes us proud. Just put on another layer and get out there. Take a look around next winter. The bike paths and streets are still full of bikes, pedaled by riders bulbous with gear to ward off the chill. Big, burly steeds with names like Pugsley plow furrows through new snow leading to the office or coffeeshop or bike shop. You just know there's a smile behind that icicle-fringed balaclava. The flip side of our winters is, well, the other six months of the year—warm-weather riding that can be short-lived, but what a glorious time it is. Spring can be finicky, with unpredictable days of cold, wet, and wind, but it is an easygoing transition time, in step with emerging flowers and leaves and a rising thermometer. Summer days are typically perfect, with temps around 80°F, but watch out for bouts of stifling humidity when it feels like you can grab handfuls of air and you sweat buckets just reaching down to tie a shoe. With red-orange-yellow proclamations, the sauna-like conditions are cleansed by crisp fall air settling over apple festivals and corn on the cob and family picnics. More than a few of your brethren will declare this the best riding season of them all, and it's hard to argue when you coast down a sinuous ribbon of tarmac unrolling through a deep crease in a bluff, smoldering in fiery autumn dress.

"Oh ya, you betcha, fer sure, doncha know." Grab a buddy, corral the kids, hop on your bikes, and go for a ride in America's best bike city. There's never been a better time.

# How to Use This Guide

The rides in this book were chosen by their best qualities to represent some of the best places for Twin Cities cycling. I included downtown and suburban routes and a few rides out in the country. All rides are within the metro or roughly an hour's drive. Each route is introduced with the traditional guidebook fare of location, distance, highlights, GPS coordinates, and other vital information, followed by a narrative of the ride, including what to expect, local history, area bike shops and restaurants, and sidebars with bonus nuggets. All of this will help you choose which rides are best before heading out:

**Start:** Starting location of the ride

**Distance:** Miles from start to finish

**Riding time:** Strong, skilled riders may be able to do a given ride in less than the estimated time; other riders may take considerably longer. Also bear in mind that severe weather, changes in trail conditions, or mechanical problems may prolong a ride.

**Best bike:** Best gear for the terrain—road, mountain, hybrid, or cyclocross bike

**Terrain and surface type:** A look at what to expect for ups and downs, and on what kind of surface (smooth road, choppy road, dirt singletrack, etc.)

**Highlights:** Special features or qualities that make the ride worth doing (as if we needed an excuse!); cool things to see along the way, historical notes, neighboring attractions

**Hazards:** Anything with the potential to disrupt your ride, like traffic, a huge pothole, busy train crossing, too many ice-cream shops

**Other considerations:** Anything extra specific to the ride, like debris on the trail after a heavy rain

**Maps:** US Geological Survey (USGS) maps are noted for each ride, along with any other worthy maps. (**Note:** The maps in the book are for general navigation only. Always be prepared with an updated map or accurate directions before heading out.)

**Getting there:** How to reach the trailhead from a major nearby location, including GPS coordinates

Note that riding time is just that—the time your bike is actually moving. Allow more time for rest or scenic stops, and of course for speed. Slower riders will naturally spend more time on the road than go-fast racers. Some riders stop for lunch; others hammer start to finish, hardly coming up for air. GPS coordinates are included for all trailheads and some key photo locations of superlative viewing sites or other notable route landmarks.

Remember, the real world is always in flux, and road conditions and trail routes might look completely different, or be gone altogether, in the time it took this book to make it into your hands. Mountain bike trails, especially, are in an almost constant state of rebuilding, rerouting, or other modification. I know of two trails in the south metro alone that had changed their tune before I even finished the first round of edits. Always plan ahead, and refer to detailed maps before hitting the road or trail.

After the ride specs comes **The Ride**, a few paragraphs of description that focus on highlights you can expect to encounter along the ride. This is followed by **Miles and Directions**, a detailed mile-by-mile description of the ride. These turn-by-turn directions allow for efficient route planning, but your own variations (detours, rest stops, side trips) along with terrain, riding technique, and even tire pressure can affect odometer readings and skew the whole works, so consider the mileages listed as a solid, but not bulletproof, reference.

# Safety

In some areas of the Twin Cities, the terrain can change drastically from one mile to the next. Even on "easy" and flat routes, it is important to be ready before you ride. Flying out the door in March for a century ride will shock your off-season, leaden legs into an abrupt and painful revolt. Put in plenty of base miles for a solid fitness level ahead of time, and know your limits. Clean rims, brakes, handlebars, seat, shifters, derailleurs, and chain to make sure they survived the last trip and are functioning properly. Get into this habit after your ride, as well.

A helmet is essential for cycling. It can prevent serious injuries—even save your life. My face landed on a log one day on a mountain bike ride, and thanks to my helmet I left the scene with only a big knot on my head instead of taking a stroll through the Pearly Gates. Don't ride without one. Cycling gloves are another indispensable piece of safety equipment that can save your hands from cuts and bruises from falls, encroaching branches, and rocks. They also improve your grip and comfort on the handlebars.

Always pack or carry at least one full water bottle. On longer rides, don't leave the house without two (or even three) bottles, or plan your ride so that it passes someplace where potable water is available. (Most every ride in this book passes relatively close to a convenience store or other oasis.) A snack or energy bars will keep your quads cranking for extra hours and prevent the dreaded "bonk"—the sudden loss of energy when your body runs out of fuel. Dress for the weather, and if it looks suspect, pack a jacket that repels both wind and water to prevent a truly horrible and potentially dangerous ride. Don't forget sunglasses, sunscreen (use the sports stuff that won't run down into your eyes and mouth), lip balm, and insect repellent for the fat tire rides—especially critical in early- to midsummer riding in Minnesota, especially near the rivers.

A basic tool kit can save you from a long walk home or further damage to your bike. A tire pump or $CO_2$ cartridge and tube patch kit are vital, and a few other tools can make the difference between disaster and a 5-minute pit stop. Carry an all-in-one tool for tightening or adjusting seat post, handlebars, chainrings, pedals, brake posts, and other components. While I generally carry just a minimum, some folks aren't comfortable unless they bring a whole shop's worth of tools. They're weighted down, and wrenches rattle with every bump in the trail, but they are rarely stranded by mechanical failures.

# Ride Finder

## RIVER CRUISES
1 Downtown Sampler
8 Minnesota River Greenway
11 Saint Paul Harbor River Tour
12 Saint Paul Grand Round
14 Big Rivers and Lilydale
15 Grey Cloud Island

## RAIL-TRAIL RAMBLERS
2 City and Lakes Loop
4 Dakota Rail Regional Trail—Lake Minnetonka Loop
6 Luce Line State Trail to Stubbs Bay
13 Gateway and Browns Creek State Trails

## CITY TOURS
1 Downtown Sampler
2 City and Lakes Loop
3 Grand Rounds
11 Saint Paul Harbor River Tour
12 Saint Paul Grand Round

## SUBURBAN EXPLORERS
4 Dakota Rail Regional Trail—Lake Minnetonka Loop

## PARKS AND RESERVES
5 Elm Creek Park Reserve
7 Hyland Park Trails

# FAT TIRE LIGHT (EASYGOING MOUNTAIN BIKE TRAILS)

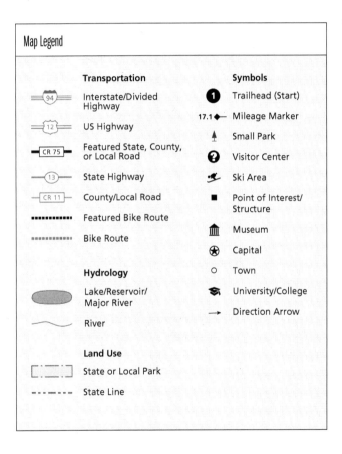

## Map Legend

### Transportation

≡94≡ Interstate/Divided Highway

≡12≡ US Highway

■CR 75■ Featured State, County, or Local Road

─13─ State Highway

─CR 11─ County/Local Road

▪▪▪▪▪▪▪▪ Featured Bike Route

▪▪▪▪▪▪▪▪ Bike Route

### Hydrology

Lake/Reservoir/ Major River

River

### Land Use

State or Local Park

State Line

### Symbols

❶ Trailhead (Start)

17.1◆ Mileage Marker

🏕 Small Park

❷ Visitor Center

🎿 Ski Area

■ Point of Interest/ Structure

🏛 Museum

✪ Capital

○ Town

🎓 University/College

→ Direction Arrow

# Minneapolis Road and Pathways

The City of Lakes does its riding residents proud with nearly 200 combined miles of on- and off-street bike lanes and trails. Much of this mileage is centered along water, around which Minneapolis was born and prospered, be it lakes, rivers, or streams. Sinuous pathways trace the banks of the mighty Mississippi River, from the historical downtown mill ruins south through forested limestone bluffs. Cyclists can linger all day long in the city, rolling along the Greenway through one of the hottest restaurant and arts scenes in the country, ride with the vibe of the lively college scene at the University of Minnesota campus, take in vibrant neighborhood festivals, or kick back on an overlook high above the river. A popular summertime destination is the chain of lakes just south of downtown, with well-traveled pathways circling a foursome of tree-lined lakes highlighted by Lakes Calhoun and Harriet, with sailing races, kite festivals, live music at the bandshell, and good old-fashioned days of fun in the sun.

A wooded corridor spurs off the south end of Lake Harriet like a long tail of a letter Q, and riders can follow the curves, twists, and meanders of Minnehaha Creek all the way to its namesake park and falls at the eastern edge of the city. Other trails mirror the spokes of your wheels, radiating to neighboring towns on routes like the Cedar Lake and LRT Trails, passing homegrown coffee and ice-cream shops along the way. Enjoy watching wildlife? Wander through Elm Creek and Hyland Parks to spot dozens of species of flora and fauna, many of them native to Minnesota. And miles of open country roads await in suburbs to the west and south, for easy spins or all-day epics.

# 1 Downtown Sampler

A short spin around the city might be just what you need to put some spring in your step. This 3.8-mile sampler tour rolls right through the heart of downtown and loops past the University of Minnesota to cross the Mississippi for a perfect start to this day or weekend cruise.

**Start:** Central Mississippi Riverfront Park
**Distance:** 3.8-mile loop
**Riding time:** About 45 minutes
**Best bike:** Road or hybrid
**Terrain and surface type:** Flat, paved city streets and pathways
**Highlights:** Hennepin Avenue Bridge, old Main Street, U of M action, Mississippi River

**Hazards:** Use caution at all road crossings; stay alert for damage to pathways (potholes, washouts, big cracks).
**Other considerations:** Pathways can get crowded on summer weekends. Watch for errant riders.
**Map:** USGS Minneapolis South

**Getting there:** From I-35, take the Washington Avenue exit and head west to Portland Avenue. Turn right and reach the Stone Arch Bridge in 2 blocks. Follow the park road to the right, about 0.25 mile to the parking area and trailhead. GPS: N44 97.917' / W93 25.441'

## The Ride

Progeny of glacial Lake Itasca in northern Minnesota, the Mississippi River is the state's iconic waterway, steeped in timeless history and inspiration to Native Americans; industrial pioneers; and nature-loving, adventurous spirits. Minneapolis and Saint Paul are closely tied siblings with very distinct and proud personalities, and while the river marks a

## OL' MISS

Minnesota's most prodigious export, the **Mississippi River** watershed, the second largest in the world, extends from the Allegheny Mountains to the Rockies, draining thirty-one states from its tranquil origin at Lake Itasca to the wide delta exit into the Gulf of Mexico. Minnesota claims the Mississippi's narrowest point, at the 25-foot-wide headwaters, and naturally occurring widest, over the 2-mile span of Lake Pepin. On this trail ride along the river's urban wilderness stretch through the Twin Cities, look to the trees and skyward for myriad songbirds, bald eagles, and red-tailed hawks.

fluid boundary between the two, its dynamic spoils also hold them together. This ride starts at Central Mississippi Riverfront Park and follows car-free trails past Mill Ruins Park and the Stone Arch Bridge, within sight of the city's birthplace. A short way further on, the route switchbacks up a bike ramp to Hennepin Ave. where you'll cross the bridge toward the iconic Grain Belt Beer sign, and then take a hard right down to Merriam Street.

This is a beautiful part of the city, with Nicollet Island Park, its namesake pavilion, and the venerable Nicollet Island Inn. Cross the old trestle bridge to Main Street for a fun trip cruising among the shops and patio restaurants. *Hot tip:* This area is especially cool at night, all lit up in a glow of lights, with amazing views of the downtown skyline.

Ride past St. Anthony Falls and Hennepin Island Park to Sixth Avenue and up to University Avenue. Cruise the bike path to the outskirts of the U of M's East Bank at East River Road and follow the pathways to the old No. 9 railroad bridge, with drop-dead views upstream and down. Across the bridge, look for the first right turn path leading down

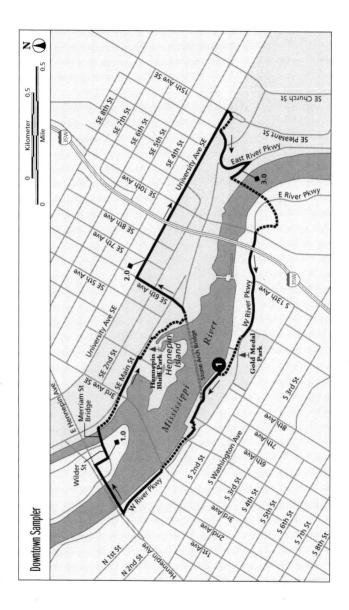

Downtown Sampler

to West River Parkway. Follow the parkway path past the Guthrie Theater and back to the trailhead.

## Miles and Directions

**0.0** Ride west from the trailhead toward the Stone Arch Bridge, following the path the Third Avenue / Central Avenue bridge.

**0.7** Junction with Hennepin Avenue bridge. Follow the bike ramp to street level and cross the river.

**0.8** Turn right on Island Avenue and drop down to Merriam Street. Cross the trestle bridge to Main Street.

**1.0** Right turn on Main Street, following the bike path past Central Avenue and through the fun woods trail.

**1.6** Junction with Sixth Avenue; turn left.

**1.8** Right turn at University Avenue.

**2.4** Right turn at East River Road. Follow the pathways for 0.3 mile to the trail leading to the No. 9 bridge and head across. Enjoy great views from the bridge!

**3.0** Turn right on the path through the woods to West River Parkway. Follow the parkway back to the trailhead.

**3.8** Arrive back at the trailhead.

## Ride Information

### RESTAURANTS

Jump-start with java and a huge muffin at **Dunn Brothers Coffee**, 329 W. 15th St.; (612) 872-4410; dunnbrothers.com.

Overindulge after the ride with Italian decadence at **Buca di Beppo**, 1204 Harmon Place; (612) 288-0138; bucadibeppo.com.

## BIKE SHOP

For more than three decades, legions of Twin Cities cyclists have made **Freewheel Bike Shop** their go-to shop. Passionate staff at their flagship West Bank, Midtown Bike Center (on the Greenway), and Eden Prairie locations bring their love of the sport to customers and to the road. Midtown is a popular commuter hub close to everything, with storage, rentals, public repair shop, and cafe. Main store at 1812 S. Sixth St., Minneapolis; (612) 339-2219; freewheelbike.com.

# 2 City and Lakes Loop

The City and Lakes Loop shows off a highlight reel of historic and new attractions in Minneapolis and points west, following some of the city's most popular bike trails. Cruise the lakes area, the Midtown Greenway, and downtown's riverfront. Plan your ride right and catch a Twins game at Target Field on your way by.

**Start:** Downtown Minneapolis or Hopkins. This trailhead option is at the Depot Coffee House in Hopkins, 9451 Excelsior Boulevard.

**Distance:** 22.7-mile loop

**Riding time:** 1.5-2 hours

**Best bike:** Road or hybrid

**Terrain and surface type:** Flat to gently rolling bike path and roadways

**Highlights:** Mid-ride goodies at Birchwood Cafe, great downtown skyline views, superb metro trail system loop, Lake Calhoun attractions, Mississippi River views, downtown Mill and Warehouse Districts, Target Field

**Hazards:** Traffic at road crossings, crowded pathways on summer weekends

**Other considerations:** Potential for extra traffic on game days at Target Field; Greenway and Cedar Lake trails attract a diverse group of riders (blazing fast to slow and squirrely) and other trail users.

**Map:** USGS Hopkins

**Getting there:** Exit US 169 at Excelsior Boulevard. Depot Coffee House is 0.1 mile east of US 169. GPS: N44 55.434' / W93 23.962'

## The Ride

As you fuel up with organic, locally roasted coffee and a sandwich at the Depot, take a minute to reflect on this neighborhood landmark. A busy rail hub on the Minneapolis and St. Louis Railway line for nearly one hundred years, the 1902 depot continues its service today as a unique community project. Ambitious student volunteers from the Hopkins School District planned the renovation and staff it seven days a week, providing a place to learn and hang out in a positive environment. A bonus for young kids and train buffs: There is a Canadian Pacific switching yard just west of the depot, where big locomotives prepare for a hard day's work.

Start the ride heading north from the depot and connect with the Cedar Lake Trail on the north side of Excelsior Boulevard, warming up with an arrow-straight 3 miles through nondescript urban scenery. Use caution at street crossings of Blake Road, Wooddale Avenue, and Beltline Boulevard. A bend finally appears in the path as it nears Lake Calhoun, and at about 4 miles the route reaches the junction with the Kenilworth Trail and an optional mileage variation. The Kenilworth Trail leads north between Lake of the Isles and Cedar Lake and past the elegant, historic homes of the Kenwood neighborhood to the northern spur of the Cedar Lake Trail. This effectively cuts the loop in half for shorter rides on either side of the lakes area.

The Kenilworth junction also marks the transition to the Midtown Greenway, the wildly popular 5.5-mile corridor trail stretching from Uptown to the Mississippi River. Also a former railroad line, the Greenway is a major transportation thruway for the self-propelled, supported by the active Midtown Greenway Coalition, which helps maintain the trail and sponsors all sorts of cool events year-round. The trail is even plowed in winter to accommodate the city's stalwart cyclists.

Less than 0.5 mile east of the lakes, the trail passes the vibrant Uptown area and then continues eastbound and across Hiawatha Avenue over the stunning Martin Olav Sabo

Bridge. At West River Parkway is the start of a scenic section of parks and river views from the bike path following the ridge above the river.

Reaching I-35W, the trail passes the Remembrance Garden, the I-35W bridge collapse memorial. As you ride into downtown, the trail enters the historic Mill Ruins district and heads back to the trailhead along I-394.

## Miles and Directions

**0.0** Start at the trailhead and follow the Cedar Lake Trail north past Excelsior Boulevard. Turn east, heading toward downtown.

**4.3** Junction with Kenilworth Trail. Continue straight ahead onto the Midtown Greenway.

**5.1** Pass Lake of the Isles and Uptown.

**7.1** Pass the Midtown Bike Center.

**8.3** Sabo bridge crossing at Hiawatha Avenue.

**8.8** Left turn onto 30th Avenue.

**9.6** Right turn onto East 25th Street.

**9.8** Rest stop at Birchwood Cafe.

**9.9** Left turn onto 35th Avenue.

**10.0** Turn right onto 24th Avenue then left onto West River Parkway.

**13.2** Pass under I-35, and the Remembrance Garden.

**13.3** Ride through Mill Ruins Park and downtown riverfront.

**13.4** Pass Stone Arch Bridge.

**14.7** Ride under Hennepin Avenue bridge.

**14.9** Left turn onto Cedar Lake Trail.

**15.6** Pass Target Field.

**17.2** Pass the Kenilworth Trail.

**19.2** Pass under MN 100.

**22.7** Arrive back at the trailhead.

# City and Lakes Loop

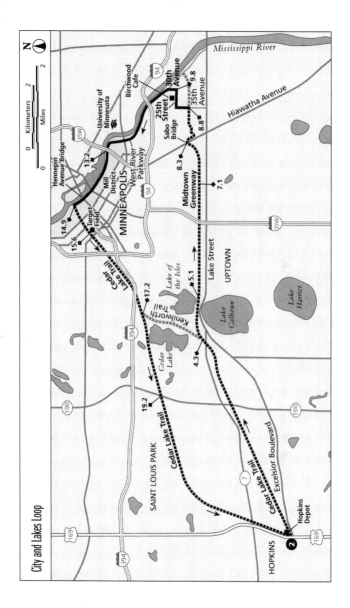

# Ride Information

## RESTAURANTS

Organic produce, free-range eggs, and fair-trade coffee high-light **Birchwood Cafe**'s homegrown approach to a good meal. The former dairy and neighborhood grocery also sponsors a bike racing team and a biyearly cleanup day on the Greenway. 3311 E. 25th St.; (612) 722-4474; birchwoodcafe .com.

Perennial best-in-Minnesota award winner **Pizza Lucé** makes unforgettable handmade gourmet pies, with a con-venient location right off the Cedar Lake Trail for post-ride indulgence. 210 N. Blake Rd., Hopkins; (952) 767-0804; pizzaluce.com.

## AREA EVENTS AND ATTRACTIONS

Fund-raising was never so much fun. The **Greenway Glow/ Northern Spark** is part art show, part rolling party to cel-ebrate bikes and raise moola for the Midtown Greenway Coalition. Light up your bike and ride the Greenway at night. Second week in June; midtowngreenway.org.

# 3  Grand Rounds

The Grand Rounds Scenic Byway explores the best of Minneapolis's copious scenery, culture, and history on a collection of manicured parkways, bike paths, and quiet streets through the city's seven byway districts. Ain't it grand?

**Start:** Minnehaha Park, at 4801 Minnehaha Park Drive
**Distance:** The Grand Rounds comprise 50 total miles. This 12.8-mile out-and-back follows parts of the main 33-mile parkway route. Many longer and shorter options are available.
**Riding time:** About 1 hour for featured ride
**Best bike:** Road or hybrid
**Terrain and surface type:** Flat and gently rolling paved pathways and roads

**Highlights:** Downtown riverfront, Mississippi River bluffs, city lakes scene, wildflower gardens, military memorials
**Hazards:** Use caution at all road crossings; watch for traffic on city streets.
**Other considerations:** Plan on extra time to see the sights; pack extra food and water, and bring a camera.
**Map:** USGS Saint Paul West

**Getting there:** From downtown Minneapolis, follow MN 55 (Hiawatha Avenue) south to the park. From MN 62 (Crosstown Highway), near MSP International Airport, follow MN 55 north to the park. GPS: N44 55.026' / W93 12.692'

## The Ride

Much of America's richest natural and cultural rewards survive today thanks to farsighted visionaries from the past. Horace Cleveland, a landscape gardener for the city of

## MINNEHAHA PARK DISTRICT

Minnehaha Creek begins its 22-mile journey from Grays Bay in Lake Minnetonka, and it saves its best for the sinuous stretch from Lake Harriet to the Mississippi River, the finale of this version of the Grand Rounds loop. Never leaving sight of the clear and gently flowing stream, the recreation paths and parkway wind past idyllic picnic areas, stately homes, and vibrant neighborhoods on the way to Lake Nokomis, host to summer weekend sailboat races, canoeing, swimming, and cruising the parkways. Ride past the lake and follow Minnehaha Parkway to its namesake park; relax with a treat from the ice-cream truck and a view of 50-foot Minnehaha Falls. The Grand Rounds Information Center is close by, adjacent to the falls at the historic Longfellow House.

Minneapolis park system in the late 1800s, urged city officials to look forward and preserve the area's ample outdoor attractions. His inspiration sparked what is now the country's premier national scenic byway and a veritable playground for cyclists. Informational kiosks and signed routes lead riders past a dozen lakes and a couple of waterfalls, through parks and wildflower gardens, big city bustle and quiet neighborhoods. More than fifty interpretive sites also dot the loop, showing off our city's best in exhibits and historical sites, such as the Longfellow House, historic Main Street, and Mill Ruins Park. You can throw a dart anywhere at a map of the Grand Rounds to start this highlight reel ride. With so many options to satisfy your every two-wheeled desire, the fun is all up to you!

This ride starts at Minnehaha Falls to follow the Mississippi upstream to the Stone Arch Bridge for an enjoyable out-and-back jaunt.

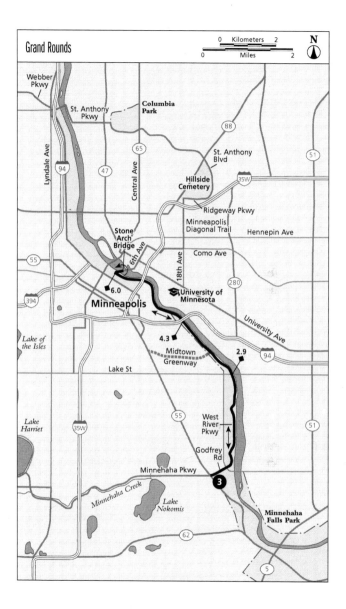

Grand Rounds

Webber Pkwy

St. Anthony Pkwy

Columbia Park

Lyndale Ave

94

65

47

Central Ave

88

51

St. Anthony Blvd

35W

Hillside Cemetery

Ridgeway Pkwy

Minneapolis Diagonal Trail

Hennepin Ave

Stone Arch Bridge

6th Ave

18th Ave

Como Ave

55

**6.0**

**Minneapolis**

University of Minnesota

280

University Ave

394

Lake of the Isles

**4.3**

Midtown Greenway

**2.9**

94

Lake St

55

Lake Harriet

35W

West River Pkwy

51

Godfrey Rd

**3**

Minnehaha Pkwy

Minnehaha Creek

Lake Nokomis

Minnehaha Falls Park

62

5

0 Kilometers 2

0 Miles 2

N

# Miles and Directions

**0.0**  Start at the trailhead at the Minnehaha Falls Park pavilion. Head east along Godfrey Road and north on the bike path, following West River Parkway.

**1.8**  Pass horseshoe bend at Mississippi Park.

**2.9**  Pass underneath Lake Street.

**3.3**  Junction with Midtown Greenway Trail. Continue straight ahead.

**4.3**  Pass beneath the I-94 bridge and enjoy great views of the U of M campus.

**5.2**  Pass the U of M West Bank Campus to your left and the Bohemian Flats area. The trail curves northwest to pass beneath I-35W.

**6.0**  Arrive at Mill Ruins Park and Mill District. Continue on the path.

**6.4**  Junction with Portland Avenue and the Stone Arch Bridge. Return the way you came.

**12.8**  Arrive back at the trailhead.

# Ride Information

## RESTAURANTS

Got a sudden urge for seafood? Skip the Clif Bar and try oysters on the half shell or crab chowder from **Sea Salt Eatery**. Top it off with a scoop of hometown favorite Sebastian Joe's ice cream to make this a perfect day. Open Apr–Oct. 4801 Minnehaha Ave. S; (612) 721-8990; seasalteatery.wordpress .com.

## AREA EVENTS AND ATTRACTIONS

The **Minneapolis Aquatennial Festival** began delighting visitors in 1940 with the festively competitive milk carton boat races and the Torchlight Parade. Mid-July in downtown; aquatennial.com.

The **Lyndale Park Rose Garden** is the second oldest of its kind in the country. Don't miss the rainbow colors of blooms from mid-June to early October. Also on the grounds is the Roberts Bird Sanctuary, home to migratory and nesting birds like warblers and great horned owls. Located at the northeast corner of Lake Harriet.

# 4 Dakota Rail Regional Trail–Lake Minnetonka Loop

To the delight of cycling fans, the Minnetonka-area trail system added the Dakota Rail Trail in 2009, treating riders to a flat cruise between Wayzata and St. Bonifacius. This 22-mile route combines the rail trail with a squiggly scenic tour of the neighborhoods around Lake Minnetonka. Don't-miss stops include the Minnetonka Drive-In, Noerenberg Gardens, historic Wayzata Train Depot, and boat watching on the lake.

**Start:** Wayzata swimming beach park at 175 Grove Lane in Wayzata

**Distance:** 22.5-mile loop

**Riding time:** 2–2.5 hours

**Best bike:** Road or hybrid

**Terrain and surface type:** Flat to rolling on paved path and city streets

**Highlights:** Noerenberg Gardens, train depot, great lake views, Minnetonka Drive-In

**Hazards:** Light traffic on neighborhood streets (busier on weekends); use caution at road crossings.

**Other considerations:** Trail will be busy on weekends, especially from Wayzata to Mound.

**Map:** USGS Excelsior

**Getting there:** Follow I-394 west of I-494 to MN 101. Head south to Lake Street and west to Grove Lane into the beach parking lot. GPS: N44 58.154' / W93 3 1.153'

## The Ride

Legions of lake lovers descend upon Wayzata Beach to soak up the sun, build a sand castle, or launch into the water to start a triathlon or other uber-endurance event, like the 9-mile Open Water Championship. Swimming to some point too far away to see land sounds, well, far. Let's stick to two wheels and follow the short access street westbound from the beach, across Shoreline Drive, and onto the Dakota Rail Trail. The silky smooth path parallels Shoreline Drive for the entire first stretch of this ride, passing scenic marshes and bays near Browns Bay and Tanager Lake. Right around 3 miles is the junction with North Shore Drive, which leads away from the lake to Noerenberg Memorial Gardens. This is the former estate of Grain Belt Brewery founder Frederick Noerenberg. His 1890 Queen Anne–style home was one of the first permanent homes on Lake Minnetonka, and its

## TONKA TOYS

All respectable kids worth their weight in slingshots and squirt guns always had a big ol' Tonka Toy in their backyard sandbox. These rough-and-tough toys built roads and pits and mountains, and plowed ditches that carried temporary rivers poured from pails. Dozers, loaders, cranes, and the burly dump truck—the crew boss. Fat black tires dirty with mud. Faded yellow paint streaked with scars of rust. A dent or two in its cavernous box made of real metal. All the while lugging payloads of sand, rocks, logs, or lesser toys with no business being in the work zone.

Generations of kids nurtured that heavy-equipment creativity thanks to three farsighted tinkerers from Mound Metalcraft. Taking inspiration from the Dakota-Sioux word *tonka* (meaning "great"), the company introduced a steam shovel and crane design to the toy market in 1947. The brawny toys were a huge hit and ushered in a sixty-five-year tradition of construction-based fun. The company changed its name to *Tonka Toys* Incorporated in 1955, and with nearly 300 million of the venerable metal toys in the hands of kids all over the world, Tonka is still king of the sandbox.

gardens are still considered one of the finest formal gardens in Minnesota.

The trail continues to a skinny spit of land between Browns and Crystal Bays, crossing the narrows over a short bridge and rounding a curve to the tony Lafayette Country Club. Keep riding into the sleepy village of Navarre, one of Lake Minnetonka's original towns, and keep heading west past Shadywood Road to the Minnetonka Drive-In for an early break. Resistance is futile when this legendary, 50-year-old landmark tempts you with a made-on-site root beer float. After spoiling your riding form, turn back east on the trail to the Tonka Bay neighborhood. Turn left at the junction with the Lake Minnetonka LRT Regional Trail. This packed, crushed limestone path is typically in great condition and, best of all, traffic-free. The path rolls into the feel-good town of Excelsior, a mid-1850s village with a solid hold on its historical roots, including a bike- and pedestrian-friendly main street.

Continue riding across the narrows between St. Albans and Excelsior Bays, paralleling Minnetonka Boulevard through Greenwood, home of the historic Old Log Theater, and eventually to the headwaters of Minnehaha Creek. It's rare to see the virgin headwaters of a stream or river, and it's pretty cool that this is the birthplace of one of the state's most famous waterways.

## Miles and Directions

**0.0** Start at the Wayzata swimming beach trailhead and follow the Dakota Rail Trail westbound.

**1.0** Pass northern shore of Browns Bay, followed by Smith Bay.

**4.0** Cross narrows at Crystal Bay and ride past the ritzy Minnetonka Beach neighborhood.

# Dakota Rail Regional Trail – Lake Minnetonka Loop

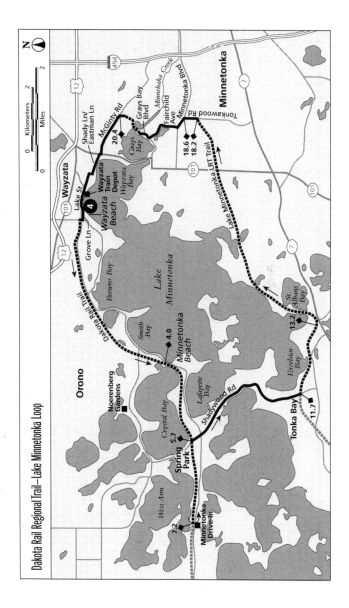

**5.7** Pass junction with Shadywood Road.

**7.2** Enjoy a root beer rest stop at the Minnetonka Drive-In. Return on the trail and head eastbound to Shadywood Road.

**8.8** Junction with Shadywood Road. Turn right, passing bay of Lake Minnetonka to village of Tonka Bay.

**11.7** Junction with Lake Minnetonka LRT Regional Trail. Turn left.

**13.2** The trail curves north, between Excelsior and Saint Albans Bays, then turns east along Minnetonka Boulevard.

**18.2** Left turn onto Tonkawood Road.

**18.5** Left turn onto Minnetonka Boulevard.

**18.6** Right turn onto Fairchild Avenue.

**19.4** Fairchild Avenue blends into Grays Bay Boulevard, continuing the route northbound.

**19.8** At the back side of the cul-de-sac, follow the bike path bridge across the headwaters of Minnehaha Creek.

**20.1** Ride north on Crosby Road to McGinty Road.

**20.4** Turn left onto McGinty Road.

**21.2** Junction with MN 101. Continue west on Shady Lane then Eastman Lane to East Lake Street.

**21.7** Left turn onto East Lake Street.

**22.5** Left turn onto Grove Lane; arrive back at the trailhead.

---

Did you know? The prolific boogie-woogie harmony trio the Andrews Sisters grew up in Mound and retained close ties with their hometown throughout their career. The city honored the girls with the Andrews Sisters Trail, a brick-and-paved pathway along Lost Lake.

# Ride Information

## RESTAURANTS

Family-owned for fifty years and counting, the **Minnetonka Drive-In** still serves up mouthwatering burgers and made-on-site root beer. Don't miss Hot Rod and Classic Car nights on summer Thursday evenings. 4658 Shoreline Dr., Spring Park; (952) 471-9383; minnetonkadrivein.com.

## BIKE SHOP

Steve Phyle has been in and around the bike business since high school, and his **Tonka Cycle & Ski** shop has been a family favorite for more than fifty years; it's the locals' year-round go-to for bikes, skis, and snowboards.16 Shady Oak Rd., Hopkins; (952) 938-8336; tonkacycleandski.com.

# 5  Elm Creek Park Reserve

Roll on 15.0 miles of sinuous pathways through woods, marshland, and meadows and past six lakes in the largest reserve in the Three Rivers Regional Parks system. Elm Creek's 4,900 acres host more than 30 miles of trails, with connections to the Rush Creek and Medicine Lake Regional Trails. Keep an eye out for the park's resident wildlife.

**Start:** Northern trailhead access at Elm Creek and Hayden Lake Roads, adjacent to the off-leash dog park
**Distance:** 15.0-mile loop, with easy access to more miles on the Rush Creek and Medicine Lake Regional Trails
**Riding time:** 1–1.5 hours

**Best bike:** Road or hybrid
**Terrain and surface type:** Flat to gently rolling on wide, paved pathways
**Highlights:** Impeccable trails, deep woods wilderness feel, Eastman Nature Center, Pierre Bottineau House, rich variety of critters

*Winding through the woods*

**Hazards:** Stay alert for other trail users and sudden appearance of wildlife; low-traffic residential streets when connecting to Rush Creek or Medicine Lake Trail.

**Other considerations:** Trails are busy on summer weekends.
**Maps:** USGS Anoka; Three Rivers Parks map

**Getting there:** From US 169 and I-94, head north for 5 miles on US 169 to MN 610 then west 3 miles to Fernbrook Lane. Turn right and go north 1 mile to Elm Creek Road. Turn right and follow it east 3 miles to the Hayden Lake Road trailhead. GPS: N45 10.113' / W93 25.324'

## The Ride

On the day I rode Elm Creek's trails, I saw a little girl on a squeaky trike patrolling the visitor center and two racers decked out in their team gear speeding around a turn on a perimeter trail. There was a pack of runners looking very businesslike, training for an upcoming event, and an elderly couple next to prairie wildflowers with binoculars trained on a bluebird. This confirmed what I'd always heard: Elm Creek really does have something for everyone. Whatever your plans for visiting this north metro park, pad them with some extra time. The scenery is ride-off-the-trail gorgeous, and the visitor center alone is worth a stop. With a swimming hole and on-site mountain bike trails, there is a full day of fun all over the place.

Access points for the park's trail system are dotted all around its boundary; I chose the Hayden Lake Road location for its proximity to alternate activities (mountain biking trails and dog park). Skinny and fat tires on the same day, right? Ride north on the paved road for about 100 yards to the trail crossing and turn left. The path starts right off with a cruise through an open meadow with songbirds flitting about, then curves through a shadowy copse of woods to cross Elm Creek Road. Roll along some minor elevation changes past borders of 6-foot-tall sumac trees, all the while surrounded by a landscape of meadow and scattered trees and pockets of wetlands on a gradual descent to a view-packed junction between Goose and Mud Lakes. Drop down past the southern horn of Goose Lake and up a small grade past a handsome stand of aspen on a southerly trajectory, moving from open land into a dense canopy of mixed hardwood forest that leads to the park entrance road. The trail serpentines its way to the visitor center, passing the championship-caliber disc golf course on your right.

Just around the curve from the visitor center is the Pierre Bottineau House, as resplendent today as it surely was in the 1800s. Imagine the great adventurer Monsieur Bottineau planning his next exploration from his outpost here in the wilds of a largely unknown territory. Today, continue across a bridge over Elm Creek and then north on an initial, arrow-straight trail past 10-foot-tall sumacs and wetlands loud with birdcalls. The path soon climbs into a wildflower-strewn

## FRENCH LINEAGE

Perched on a hill adjacent to the park's main entrance, the restored *Pierre Bottineau* House looks over the historic stomping grounds of a legendary Minnesota frontiersman.

Born of French-Canadian and half-Sioux Ojibwe blood, Bottineau was equally capable of hand-hewing a boat, romancing ladies, or leading explorations of trackless wilderness. He was an intrepid voyageur, and his travels through the wild corridor northwest of the present-day Twin Cities opened the area to settlement and forged Minnesota into a prosperous state.

meadow packed with butterflies, bluebirds, goldfinches, and cardinals. The laudable efforts of the park's forestry, wildlife, and water resources teams are evident throughout the ride. Eighty percent of the park is managed or retained in its natural state, and officials are constantly striving to preserve wildlife and rare plant species. It is an uplifting sight to see such a vibrant relationship thrive. Loop through the park's northern tier before angling back toward the official mountain bike trailhead, accompanied by a cornfield and meadow jammed with a Crayola palette of wildflowers.

A gentle climb leads up away from the woods to a nice view of Lemans Lake and into the woods again past a purple martin sanctuary. This is an Audubon Society Purple Martin Conservation Project, and it has done much to provide habitat for these threatened birds. Cruise through the woods and meadow again on a fun and winding homestretch to the trailhead.

## Miles and Directions

**0.0** Start at the Hayden Lake Road trailhead.

**1.0** Junction with Elm Creek Road. Head straight across.

**1.6** Pass junction with a spur trail heading east.

**2.0** Left turn at a trail junction, skirting the south shore of Goose Lake.

**3.0** Junction with James Deane Parkway. Ride across to continue on the bike path.

**4.0** Pass the chalet/visitor center.

**4.5** Roll past the Bottineau House.

**4.6** Junction with the Medicine Lake Regional Trail and info-packed kiosk with maps of area trails.

**6.8** Left turn at trail junction.

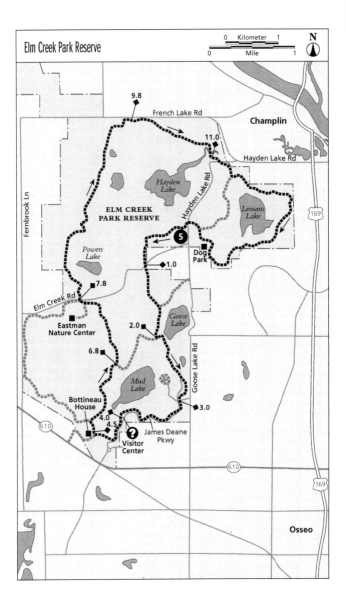

Elm Creek Park Reserve

0 Kilometer 1

0 Mile 1

N

Champlin

French Lake Rd

9.8

11.0

Hayden Lake Rd

Hayden Lake

Hayden Lake Rd

ELM CREEK
PARK RESERVE

Lemans
Lake

Fernbrook Ln

169

Powers
Lake

5

Dog
Park

1.0

7.8

Elm Creek Rd

Eastman
Nature Center

2.0

Goose
Lake

6.8

Goose Lake Rd

Mud
Lake

Bottineau
House

3.0

610

4.0
4.5

?
Visitor
Center

James Deane
Pkwy

610

169

Osseo

| **7.8** | Cross Elm Creek Road. |
| **9.8** | Briefly parallel French Lake Road. |
| **11.0** | Ride past the northern mountain bike trailhead. |
| **15.0** | Arrive back at trailhead. |

# Ride Information

### RESTAURANTS

Head to the **Lookout Bar & Grill** for homemade-good grub and a seat on Maple Grove's largest outdoor patio. Family-owned since 1958, the local favorite hosts volleyball, horseshoes, and live music. 8672 Pineview Lane N; (763) 424-4365; lookoutbarandgrill.com.

### AREA EVENTS AND ATTRACTIONS

The **PurpleRideStride** raises awareness and funds for pancreatic cancer. Ride routes follow various loops in the Maple Grove area, including Elm Creek Park; http://support .pancan.org.

# 6  Luce Line State Trail to Stubbs Bay

A Minnesota rail-trail gem, the multiuse Luce Line traces a 63-mile route from cul-de-sacs to tumbleweeds, following the path of the former Electric Short Line Railroad. This stretch passes through maple woodland and remnant tallgrass prairie with a quiet country road feel, great views, and plentiful wildlife.

**Start:** Vicksburg Lane and 10th Avenue North in Plymouth
**Distance:** 14.2 miles out and back
**Riding time:** About 1 hour
**Best bike:** Hybrid, road bike with wider tires, or cyclocross bike
**Terrain and surface type:** Flat ride on crushed limestone surface

**Highlights:** Flat, easygoing ride; Wood-Rill Scientific and Natural Area (SNA), great open country views, lots of mileage options
**Hazards:** Use caution at road crossings; stay alert for wildlife on the trail.
**Map:** USGS Hopkins

**Getting there:** From I-494 in Plymouth, exit onto CR 6; head west 1.4 miles to Vicksburg Lane and turn left. Parking and the trailhead are about 0.4 mile south at 10th Avenue. GPS: N44 59.361' / W93 28.951'

## The Ride

This longtime standby trail gained some city street cred in recent years with the 9-mile stretch from Plymouth to Minneapolis swathed in a smooth layer of pavement, including a 240-foot boardwalk over a ravine in the western section of Theodore Wirth Park. The down-to-earth stretch of

## RURAL RAILROAD

Like all rail-trail biographies, the Luce Line is steeped in history, and its westbound route from Minneapolis was an integral link to the rural reaches of early Minnesota. Built by the **Electric Short Line Railroad Company** in the early twentieth century, the line connected the prosperity of Minneapolis with the state's western farming communities.

limestone, however, stretching 60 miles to the far-off woods and prairies, feels like an Old West stagecoach track. Beyond Winsted, the path gets even more rustic, turning to gravel to crushed granite to grass. The eastern section once traveled through the immense Big Woods that blanketed this part of the state with seemingly endless stands of sugar maple, basswood, and oak. Alas, in just 200 short years, nearly 100 percent of the woods were cut down, leaving mostly scattered remnants. But about 2 miles into the ride, you'll reach a 150-acre parcel that was preserved and donated to the Minnesota Department of Natural Resources (DNR). The Wood-Rill SNA is one of the most ecologically significant in the state's compilation of natural areas, boasting trees more than 200 years old, several ponds, a tamarack swamp, and wildlife such as deer, fox, pheasant, and dozens of bird species living among the rolling hills.

Ride on past the northern bays of Lake Minnetonka and out to Watertown, known to the Dakota Indians as "Rapid Waters" and site of one of their villages. The Crow River soon attracted settlers, and the small community was named Watertown in 1858. Ride across the Crow and set your bike on cruise control through 10 arrow-straight miles of bits and pieces of the once-spectacular tallgrass prairie that grew

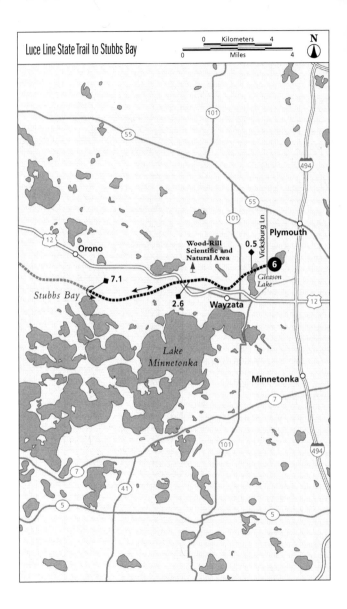

Luce Line State Trail to Stubbs Bay

0 Kilometers 4
0 Miles 4

N

55 101

494

55

101

Vicksburg Ln

Plymouth

12 Orono

Wood-Rill
Scientific and
Natural Area

0.5

6

Gleason Lake

7.1

Stubbs Bay

2.6 Wayzata

12

Lake
Minnetonka

Minnetonka

7

7

101

494

41

5

5

here. Loop around to Mill Reserve Park on the west shore of Winsted Lake for a swim, then retrace your track back to Plymouth.

## Miles and Directions

**0.0** Start at the Vicksburg Lane trailhead in Plymouth.

**0.5** Cross a cool trestle bridge over a peninsula of Gleason Lake.

**2.6** Roll past the Wood-Rill SNA.

**3.8** Cross US 12.

**7.1** Skirt the north side of Stubbs Bay. Turn back here for the return.

**14.2** Arrive back at the trailhead.

## Ride Information

### RESTAURANTS

The **Luce Line Lodge** is a go-to favorite, serving up a long list of irresistible flatbreads and pizza and a side order of history with the Lodge's railway-past decor. 305 Lewis Ave. S, Watertown; (952) 955-1305; lucelinelodge.com.

Get a mid-ride chicken sandwich at the **Blue Note**. 320 Third St. S, Winsted; (320) 485-9698; bluenoteballroom.com.

# 7 Hyland Park Trails

This scenic park in Bloomington's western reaches has long been a favorite destination for outdoor lovers. This squiggly, 5.0-mile ride explores the shady woods and open prairies of the park, with access to Hyland Lake, the kid-favorite recreation park, and the Richardson Nature Center.

**Start:** Hyland Park is at 10145 Bush Lake Road. Start the ride from the visitor center.

**Distance:** 5.0-mile loop within the park

**Riding time:** About 45 minutes in the park, but plan for an hour or more for frequent stops to see the sights. Slot 2 hours to enjoy the entire route.

**Best bike:** Road or hybrid

**Terrain and surface type:** Flat and rolling on paved trail and roads

**Highlights:** Richardson Nature Center, Hyland Lake, recreation park, copious wildlife and frame-worthy scenery, traffic-free bliss on the river flats

**Hazards:** Watch for other trail users and wildlife in the park and light traffic on city streets.

**Maps:** USGS Bloomington, Eden Prairie

**Getting there:** From West Old Shakopee Road, follow Bush Lake Road north 1.2 miles to the park entrance. From I-494, exit onto East Bush Lake Road and head south 2.5 miles to Bush Lake Road. Hyland Park is 0.3 mile south. GPS: N44 49.441' / W93 22.374'

## The Ride

Capitalizing on what the earliest Native American residents already knew, Bloomington's first European settlers thought the riverside bluffs and rolling, wooded lands looked like a

*Interior woods at Hyland Park*

fine place to set down some roots. Influenced by the Minnesota River, the city grew as a center for flour milling and farming, and influenced by notables like Gideon Pond, the area's natural treasures were always considered. With that head start, we are fortunate today to have such a gem as

Hyland Park, a wilderness retreat right at our doorstep. With Hyland Lake as a centerpiece, the park's makeup is largely open prairie, with pockets of woods throughout and larger tracts around the borders. This ride samples both on a relaxing cruise to the northern side of the park, with a dip into the woods and optional river bluff side trip to the south.

Head out from the visitor center/play area and roll south past a nice hillside meadow to a junction at the western bulb of Hyland Lake, then ride through a small copse of woods to the upper side of the meadow. A quick hook across the entrance road and you're off to the park's northern reaches, starting with a nice little pond just below the trail, typically featuring a few different flavors of waterfowl. Birdlife is all around, with a dozen different songs drifting through the air at most any time of the day. Pass a couple of pretty stands of aspen and the entrance to Bush Lake Beach (across the road), then climb an easy grade around another meadow packed with wildflowers watched over by butterflies and dragonflies. Look out over the adjoining lowland. See that tall post with the huge nest on top? I saw the white head of a bald eagle looking out over the land last time I rode here. The regal birds frequent the park, so stay alert for a look. Bush Lake Beach was constructed in 1956 and is still a popular place to cool down the summer sizzle. The path angles along barely rolling terrain through more aspen stands and intermittent meadow to Richardson Nature Center, the largest in the park system. See live animals and raptors inside, or hike the interpretive trails through forest and prairie to spot critters in the wild, such as deer, muskrat, and fox. The center has an active event calendar, including treasure hunting and pond exploration with a park naturalist.

## QBP–KEEPING THE BIKE INDUSTRY ROLLING

At the southern end of Hyland Park is **Quality Bicycle Products**, the largest bicycle parts distributor in the industry and supplier to more than 5,000 independent dealers. Founder Steve Flagg has watched his company grow at a meteoric pace, from humble beginnings in a small St. Paul office to the current 135,000-square-foot facility in Bloomington and winner of an armload of best-of honors.

**Option:** Looking for more mileage? Keep following the path north along the road all the way to the Hyland Hills ski area entrance. There is a front-row view of the Bush Lake Ski Jump on the way in (you know you want to try it) and access for a nice loop around Normandale Lake.

## Miles and Directions

**0.0** Start at the visitor center trailhead.

**0.3** Turn right at the first junction.

**0.7** Cross the entrance road.

**0.9** Stay left, paralleling Bush Lake Road.

**1.8** Junction with the Bush Lake Beach entrance. Turn right to head to the interior of the park. *Option:* Ride one mile north to take in the sights and sounds at Richardson Nature Center.

**3.5** Turn right at this junction.

**4.0** Continue straight ahead at this junction.

**4.4** Turn left at this junction, curving around to Hyland Lake's north shore.

**5.0** Arrive back at the visitor center trailhead.

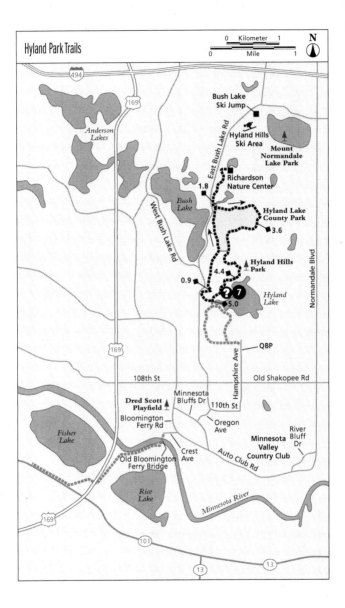

# Hyland Park Trails

0   Kilometer   1

0   Mile   1

N

I-494

US 169

US 169

108th St

Anderson
Lakes

West Bush Lake Rd

East Bush Lake Rd

Bush Lake
Ski Jump

Hyland Hills
Ski Area

Mount
Normandale
Lake Park

Richardson
Nature Center

1.8

Bush
Lake

Hyland Lake
County Park

3.6

4.4

Hyland Hills
Park

0.9

?  7

5.0

Hyland
Lake

Normandale Blvd

QBP

Hampshire Ave

Old Shakopee Rd

Dred Scott
Playfield

Minnesota
Bluffs Dr

110th St

Bloomington
Ferry Rd

Oregon
Ave

Fisher
Lake

Crest
Ave

Old Bloomington
Ferry Bridge

Auto Club Rd

Minnesota
Valley
Country Club

River
Bluff
Dr

Rice
Lake

Minnesota River

US 169

101

13

13

# Ride Information

**RESTAURANTS**

Indulge with a burger and cold brew at **Willy McCoys**. 10700 France Ave. S, Bloomington; (952) 456-8905; willy mccoys.com.

**AREA EVENTS AND ATTRACTIONS**

Guided snowshoe hikes through oak forests and open prairies at **Richardson Nature Center** in February. 8737 E. Bush Lake Rd., Bloomington; (763) 694-7676; threerivers parks.org.

For more than one hundred years, daredevil athletes have soared through the air at the **Bush Lake Ski Jump** in Bloomington. The **Minneapolis Ski Jumping Club** sponsors an active jumping club and annual tournaments, as well as "try it out" sessions for all ages. facebook.com/ mnskiclub.

# 8  Minnesota River Greenway

Cruise along the meandering Minnesota River on one of the metro's newest trails. This short out-and-back route winds through the Minnesota Valley National Wildlife Refuge and comes complete with a bike repair station and picnic area at the trailhead.

**Start:** Minnesota Riverfront Park Black Dog trailhead, on Black Dog Road east of I-35W
**Distance:** 7.4 miles out and back
**Riding time:** 45-60 minutes
**Best bike:** Road or hybrid
**Terrain and surface type:** Flat, paved path
**Highlights:** Quiet river cruise, wildlife, access to more miles at both ends of the trail

**Hazards:** Expect high water during traditional spring flooding.
**Map:** USGS Bloomington
**Getting there:** From I-35W, exit at Black Dog Road. Go east 0.2 mile to the trailhead parking area, on the north side of the road. GPS: N44 80.051' / W93 28.557 '

## The Ride

When completed, the Minnesota River Greenway will travel through Burnsville, Eagan, and Mendota Heights on its way to Lilydale Regional Park. Connector trails will deliver cyclists hither and yon through St. Paul and beyond. This short out-and-back sampler tours along the Minnesota River on silky-smooth trail.

From Minnesota Riverfront Park, ride eastbound, paralleling the river on your left and Black Dog Lake on your right. After a couple of lazy curves, the trail reaches a spur

# Minnesota River Greenway

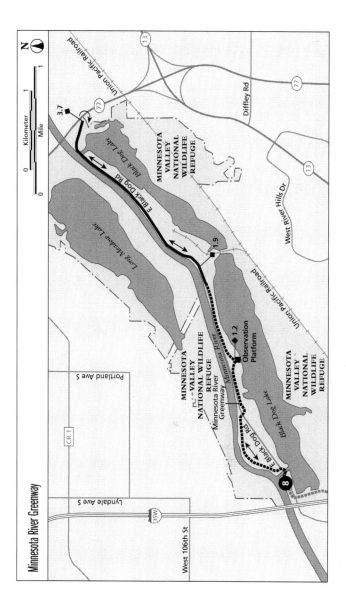

*Curving along the river*

path leading to an observation platform with beauteous views of the lake and hordes of lively wildlife. This is part of the 14,000-acre Minnesota Valley National Wildlife Refuge, a Twin Cities–area gem and one of the largest in the country. Keep an eye out for river otters, wood ducks and dozens of other waterfowl and bird species, and bald eagles overhead.

From here, keep riding east, passing the sprawling Xcel Energy plant property. Past the plant, the trail follows the roadway for the last stretch to its eastern terminus at the Cedar Avenue bridge. Don't miss riding the old road a bit and out onto the recently remodeled Old Cedar Bridge, now serving as a popular bike and walking bridge over backwaters of the Minnesota River.

Return to the Black Dog trailhead the same way you came.

## Miles and Directions

**0.0**  Start at the trailhead and ride east.

**0.8**  The trail crosses Black Dog Road.

**1.2**  Junction with path to observation deck.

**1.9**  Arrive at Xcel Energy plant. Keep following the trail/roadway.

**3.7**  Reach the Cedar Avenue bridge. Return the way you came.

**7.4**  Arrive back at the trailhead.

# Minneapolis Mountain Biking

It wasn't all that many years ago that Minnesota was hardly synonymous with destination mountain biking. With nothing resembling a high mountain or desert slickrock or coastal rain forest, adventure-seeking riders traditionally targeted the Rockies or Moab or the vast forests on either coast to fill their quota of life list trails.

That was then.

It's a whole new fat tire world here in the land of lakes, with a long list of award-winning trails packed with enough cred to stoke the fires of rookie cruisers to bridge-jumping experts to seen-it-all trail riders. Dirt lovers of every ilk will find sweet riding throughout the state. Credit for this turnaround is collectively due to the hardworking riders and local officials who sweated it out for years promoting, building, and maintaining trails, but we can zero in on one man—and one determined rider group.

Gary Sjoquist is advocacy director at Quality Bicycle Products in Bloomington, working tirelessly in the name of all that is good with our sport, with regular appearances at federal government legislation throwdowns, trade shows, and local committees. A large chunk of what you see today out on the trails can be linked in some way to Sjoquist's work and crystal-ball vision, like the sustainably constructed Lebanon Hills trails in Eagan, the nationally renowned Cuyuna State Recreation Area trails in Crosby, and a lead role in the Minnesota High School Cycling League.

Mountain bikers should also salute Minnesota Off-Road Cyclists (MORC), a nonprofit volunteer organization (cofounded by Sjoquist) dedicated to the future of fat tire riding in our state. MORC's handiwork on many of the metro area's premier trails is evident, and with their unceasing commitment, more trails continue to be added. MORC members are enthusiastically active and put in lots of trail time with tools in hand, providing unforgettable off-road riding. Check the MORC website, morcmtb.org, for a comprehensive trail list, reviews, and updates on events and volunteer opportunities.

Think mountain biking hasn't seen a similar uptick in the winter months? One look at the packed start line at winter races or any given snow-covered road or pathway will change your tune. Trail riding on a puffy layer of new snow is damn fun, and skittering along an oval track cleared from a frozen lake, with studded tires popping at the ice like miniature firecrackers and holding you right at that adrenaline-fired edge of hitting the deck . . . well, you just have to get out there and check it out.

I have included just a few of the gems in the Twin Cities area mountain bike trail collection. Yes, there are more out there, lots more. Just head out and get dirty.

# 9  Elm Creek Fat Tire Trails

Back in 2011, Three Rivers Park District and Minnesota Off-Road Cyclists (MORC) introduced 13 miles of sublime singletrack at Elm Creek, twisting around the northeast corner of the park with a perfectly blended mix of beginner to expert terrain on fast-flowing path.

**Start:** Southern trailhead at parking area across from the dog park
**Distance:** Roughly 13 miles for all loops; 7.5 miles for the intermediate loop featured here
**Riding time:** 1–1.5 hours
**Best bike:** Mountain
**Terrain and surface type:** Flat to gently rolling on hard-packed singletrack

**Highlights:** Impeccable trail conditions, fast and flowing, gorgeous scenery, relatively crowd-free
**Hazards:** Hardly an exposed root or stray branch to be seen; very worry-free trail
**Map:** USGS Anoka

**Getting there:** From US 169, head west on West Hayden Lake Road for 1.5 miles to a Y junction. Go left, following the "County Park" signs. Continue past the northern parking area 0.8 mile to the trailhead just north of the dog park. GPS: N45 16.840' / W93 43.166'

## The Ride

The two easier loops at Elm Creek, totaling a little over 2 miles, offer something you don't see every day on a mountain bike trail. The trails were designed to accommodate the wide wheelbase of three- and four-wheeled adaptive mountain bikes and hand cycles. Grades are not typically more than 5 percent, although a 900-foot-long ascent will challenge riders on Loop A. The park and MORC volunteers have done a fantastic job of constructing this trail and providing access for yet another active group of cyclists. This trail and one at Murphy-Hanrehan Park Reserve in Savage are two of the very few hand-cycle trails in the country, and the outdoor recreation staff at the park are enthusiastic for more of the same in the future. Indeed, the Twin Cities is already on its way to being the Midwest hub for adaptive mountain bike trails, with a regular and well-attended race series happening every summer.

On the trails, Loop A runs counterclockwise through a mix of open prairie and great views of surrounding wetlands and forests. Loop B is less than 1 mile with barely noticeable elevation gain, circling several ponds and tracing a squiggly glacial ridge. Both are perfect warm-up loops prior to tackling more challenging trails to the south, with the intermediate trail next up and the expert loop at the far end.

I double-dipped on my Elm Creek day and rode both the paved and dirt trails, so this route starts from the dog park trailhead. Follow the road north to the junction with the paved trail and hop on the singletrack, cruising through an open, meadowy landscape to a short climb through a chunk of woods. The route then squiggles around through the open again to meet the access to Grizzland, the expert section dotted with technical features like log piles and rock gardens, and boasting the most elevation gain on the trail. It's a blast in there, but for now we'll focus on a broader, intermediate skill level (like mine) and ride to the east on the mid-level trail, curving through a splintered copse of trees, into the open again, and back into a large tract of woods near Lemans Lake. The path continues this trees-clearing-trees pattern northbound along a small rise, then drops gradually down to

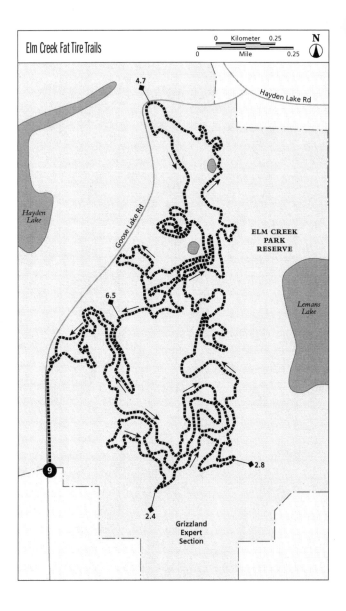

Elm Creek Fat Tire Trails

ELM CREEK
PARK
RESERVE

Hayden Lake Rd

Hayden
Lake

Goose Lake Rd

Lemans
Lake

4.7

6.5

2.8

9

2.4

Grizzland
Expert
Section

0    Kilometer    0.25

0         Mile         0.25

N

the northern trailhead. Curve around to the south and roll up and down through beautiful oak-maple-basswood forest on a fast and flowing stretch past a small pond and meadow. A "big" climb of about 70 feet takes you through more forest and around a huge meadow area to the final roller-coaster finishing straight.

## Miles and Directions

**0.0** Start at the southern trailhead and head north on the road to the paved trail.

**0.2** Hop on the singletrack leading north from the bike path.

**2.4** Junction with Grizzland. Turn left to follow the intermediate trail.

**2.8** Enter the woods on the east side of the park.

**4.7** Pass the northern trailhead.

**5.4** Pass the small pond and meadow area.

**6.5** Circle the west side of a huge, Wisconsin-shaped wetland.

**7.3** Junction with bike path and road.

**7.5** Arrive back at the trailhead.

## Ride Information

**RESTAURANTS**

Pull up a bar stool and pillage a plate of french toast or burgers and fries at **Dehn's Country Manor**, an all-in-the-family tradition since 1958. Close to the trails at 11281 Fernbrook Lane, Maple Grove; (763) 420-6460; dehnscountrymanor .com.

## AREA EVENTS AND ATTRACTIONS

**Three Rivers Parks** host a full calendar of activities throughout the year, including canoe, kayak, and stand-up paddleboard programs. Newbies can learn different paddling techniques, roll a kayak, and see what the paddleboard craze is all about. Many different flavors of events available. three riversparks.org.

# 10 **Terrace Oaks Park**

Short and fast, this entry- to intermediate-level trail winds through oak forest and wetland, with tight turns and a few punchy climbs. Ride a quick, shakedown cruise on the 2.5-mile featured loop, or scorch multiple racetrack laps to test your best times.

**Start:** Parking area and trailhead on Burnsville Parkway, 0.5 mile east of CR 11
**Distance:** 2.5-mile loop
**Riding time:** About 15 minutes
**Best bike:** Mountain
**Terrain and surface type:** Mostly rolling, with a few short, medium-steep hills on hard-packed singletrack

**Highlights:** Uncrowded, tight turns and sweeping descents, challenging expert section (optional)
**Hazards:** Encroaching foliage, handlebar-grabbing branches, turtle crossings, ticks, mosquitoes
**Map:** USGS Saint Paul SW

**Getting there:** From I-35W, exit at Burnsville Parkway and head east 2 miles, past CR 11, and down the hill 0.5 mile to the park entrance. The trailhead is adjacent to the hockey rink. GPS: N44 46.464' / W93 14.345'

## The Ride

Designed by trail-building legend Gary Sjoquist, Terrace Oaks packs a lot of fat (tire) into a small package. The 230-acre city park is adorned with wonderfully gnarled old oaks and pocket wetlands, brim full of lush foliage and critters both winged and terrestrial. There is just enough technical flair—and a short expert section—to make it interesting for

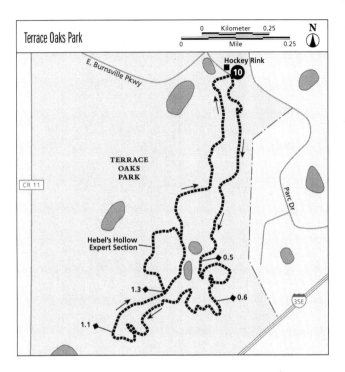

Kilometer 0.25
Mile 0.25
N

E. Burnsville Pkwy

Hockey Rink
**10**

TERRACE
OAKS
PARK

CR 11

Parc Dr

Hebel's Hollow
Expert Section

0.5

1.3

0.6

35E

1.1

more accomplished riders, as well as an easygoing feel for beginners.

Start the ride at the hockey rink and roll into densely packed woods, moving quickly to a series of twisty turns past a pair of hidden ponds, navigating past the trees in a series of hairpins and tight squiggles. Long-armed shrubbery reaches out to claw your legs through this stretch, and it's easy to scrape the bark off trailside trees, but this is a fun, keep-you-on-your-toes technical challenge. The trail is fast and flows well as it zigzags toward two pond/wetland areas, slices between them, and climbs to higher ground on a short ridge.

A nice descent drops down to the junction with the Hebel's Hollow expert section, which features a gravelly hairpin switchback and log crossing and a tightly wound, downhill switchback. The main trail continues on a lazy curve toward one more short climb and final descent to meet the entrance from the trailhead.

And just like that, you're done with a lap. Good news is, with the mountain biking hordes descending on the "money trails" like Lebanon Hills and Murphy-Hanrehan, Terrace is blissfully empty, and it often seems like your own private bike trail. Take a few laps and enjoy the peace and quiet.

## Miles and Directions

**0.0** Start at the trailhead and ride through a narrow, open area and into the woods.

**0.5** Pass the pair of ponds. Listen to the frogs.

**0.6** Curve into the twisty stretch through the trees.

**1.1** Climb up away from the ponds and loop back north.

**1.3** Junction with the Hebel's Hollow expert section. Check it out or continue down the hill.

**1.9** Junction with the entrance trail to return to the trailhead.

**2.5** Arrive back at the trailhead.

## Ride Information

### RESTAURANTS

Family-owned for upwards of fifty years, **J's Family Restaurant** still serves heaping omelets and great pizza. Just 1.5 miles north of the trailhead at 2913 Cliff Rd. E, Burnsville; (952) 890-2669.

## AREA EVENTS AND ATTRACTIONS

The **ranger programs** at the Minnesota Valley National Wildlife Refuge bring you up close to some of the best wildlife habitat in the river valley. Mid-July at the Bloomington visitor center; 3815 American Blvd.; (952) 854-5900; fws .gov/refuge/minnesota_valley.

Bloomington's ample Minnesota River frontage and its wooded bluffs were home to many generations of Native Americans. See the city's largest group of burial mounds at **Mound Springs Park**, 102nd Street and 12th Avenue, near the bluff's edge.

# Saint Paul Road and Pathways

Nearly every ride in the Saint Paul section of this book is within sight of either the Mississippi or Saint Croix River, making for superlative riding with postcard backdrops. Minnesota's capital city fits snugly around a sweeping curve of the Mississippi, flanked to the south by a rounded snout of cave-riddled limestone bluffs. Wooded corridors provide purchase for ribbons of smooth, paved trails flowing upstream and down with the river's current for long miles of scenic cruising, such as the River Tour ride from the downtown harbor to wildlife-packed Crosby Farm Park or the Big Rivers Trail in Lilydale and Mendota. The trail along Mississippi River Boulevard treats cyclists to sweet river views on the Grand Round ride and a tour of Summit Avenue, the city's most elegant address. Like to climb? Short, punchy hills shoot to the bluff tops all around St. Paul. Want more elevation gain? Head to the lumpy terrain around Newport and longer and steeper challenges near Afton. Make a day of it on the iconic Gateway Trail and the Brown's Creek segment leading to historic Stillwater, and go back in time with a double feature of Minnesota's annals in the diminutive hamlets of Marine on Saint Croix and Scandia.

# 11 Saint Paul Harbor River Tour

The Mississippi, as it does in Minneapolis, defines the personality of Saint Paul. Much of the city's most celebrated views, architecture, history, and community are influenced by the river. This entire 13-mile ride hugs the Mississippi's shoreline from water level at the downtown harbor upstream to Crosby Farm Park, with a front-row view of towboats working around the harbor and restored paddleboats motoring along the wooded bluffs.

**Start:** Riverside parking and picnic area on Warner Road, 0.2 mile east of Jackson Street

**Distance:** 13.0 miles out and back, with many options to extend or shorten

**Riding time:** About 1 hour

**Best bike:** Road or hybrid

**Terrain and surface type:** Flat to gently climbing (with one steep hill), on mostly smooth, paved pathways

**Highlights:** Riverside view of towboats in the harbor; downtown Saint Paul; Crosby Park; sinuous, water's edge trail and bluff views

**Hazards:** Watch for traffic at road junctions; prepare for downed limbs and sand on the trail through Crosby Park.

**Other considerations:** Mosquitoes will devour you on a hot midsummer evening; there are some choppy sections from past flood events.

**Map:** USGS Saint Paul East

**Getting there:** From downtown Saint Paul, follow Chestnut or Jackson Streets to the river at Shepard Road. Turn left (road becomes Warner Road) to the first large parking area at river's edge. GPS: N44 56.820' / W93 04.919'

# The Ride

The Mississippi River gets crowded in downtown Saint Paul. From the trailhead parking area along Warner Road, visitors can get up close to rumbling towboats moving barges to various staging or loading areas. On busy days, dozens of barges are docked along the riverbanks and square-framed towboats with crow's nest wheelhouses move about the harbor under the steely eyes of seasoned captains.

The sandstone river bluffs in and around Saint Paul contain a captivating labyrinth of caves and man-made mines. The granddaddy of them all was Fountain Cave, a 1,150-foot-long passageway formed by the slowly eroding path of Fountain Creek, opening into the Mississippi about halfway between present-day I-35 and the old Schmidt's Brewery. Side tunnels led to many hidden antechambers, one of them a huge, circular room, and many more still unexplored. Some of the area's caves were used for storing goods, growing mushrooms, hiding gangsters, or as sites for speakeasies. After ne'er-do-well rogue Pierre "Pig's Eye" Parrant erected the first shack at the mouth of Fountain Cave, this place spawned the growth of the city, and early residents visited the cave for its cool air and water and to explore the cave's recesses. Increased human activity, as usual, led to the cave's eventual disappearance, at least from the surface. Its entrance might be buried, but below the streets, a mysterious maze and legends still await.

Start riding upstream, following the paved path beneath the Lafayette Bridge and into the shadow of downtown's skyscrapers. Pass under Robert and Wabasha Streets and look across to Raspberry Island, home to the Minnesota Boat Club since 1870 and today host to bandshell concerts and other events. The small atoll was known as Navy Island from 1948 to about the mid-1990s, named for the US Navy training facility once housed there. Just past the bridge are great views in all directions, most notably the downtown skyline, the Science Museum of Minnesota, and Harriet Island across the river. The buff-colored pavilion at river's edge dates back to 1941 and was a popular summer destination, with a public bathhouse, beach, and picnic areas. Today the building hosts wedding ceremonies and other festive events. At the east end of Upper Landing Park, split off to the left and roll past the fountains and condo neighborhood and continue along the river, passing beneath the soaring Smith Avenue High

*View west from trailhead*

Bridge, 160 feet above. At the junction with Shepard Road proper, the route turns left and heads further west on some gently rolling sections of the Samuel Morgan Regional Trail Corridor (this is also part of the 3,000-mile-long Mississippi River Trail), passing the site of the old Fountain Cave and a flat stretch approaching I-35E. Cross the freeway ramps with caution, and in a few more pedal strokes arrive at the eastern entrance to Crosby Farm Regional Park. Roll down the hill and start the long and curvy tour of this heavily wooded park on the river flats. Named for English immigrant Thomas Crosby, who farmed the area in the late 1800s, the park today boasts nearly 7 miles of trails winding through a lush forest of immense cottonwoods and maples, Crosby Lake and wetland area, and, of course, the river. Follow the access road up the route's only steep climb, emerging at the top of the high river gorge. Pedal on to the overlook at MN 5 for great views of the river below and Fort Snelling on the other side.

Turn around, head back to the top of the Crosby Park hill, and dart out onto the Shepard Road pathway, following this all the way along the road to the Randolph Avenue junction and Shepard Road to the trailhead.

## Miles and Directions

**0.0**  Start at the trailhead at Warner Road.

**0.7**  Pass Raspberry Island.

**1.0**  Upper Landing Park. Split left.

**1.7**  Smith Avenue High Bridge.

**2.6**  Randolph Avenue and Shepard Road junction. Turn left.

**4.2**  Junction with I-35E. Continue straight ahead.

**4.3**  Junction with Crosby Farm Park. Turn left into the park.

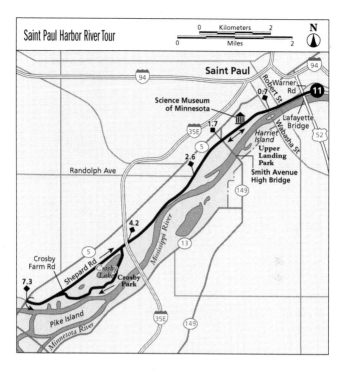

Saint Paul Harbor River Tour

**6.6**   Turn left at the picnic shelters onto the park road and head uphill.

**7.3**   Fort Snelling and river gorge overlook. Turn around here for return trip.

**7.5**   Turn left at top of the hill, onto the path paralleling Shepard Road.

**9.3**   Pass back under I-35E.

**11.4**   Randolph Avenue junction. Go straight ahead, following the path all the way back to the trailhead.

**13.0**   Arrive back at the trailhead.

# Ride Information

## RESTAURANTS

Load up on scrumptious buckwheat pancakes at **Day by Day Cafe**, a five-time award winner for best home cooking in the Twin Cities. 477 W. Seventh St.; (651) 227-0654; daybyday.com.

Got the urge? Fix it at **Caribou Coffee**'s trailside shop at Upper Landing. Do the right thing and enjoy their delicious Rainforest Alliance–certified coffee. 230 Spring St.; (651) 293-1612.

## AREA EVENTS AND ATTRACTIONS

Get your outdoor groove on at the **Twin Cities Jazz Festival** at Mears Park. Late June at Mears Park, 221 E. Fifth St., Saint Paul; twincitiesjazzfestival.com.

Bavarian-born Jacob Schmidt moved to Saint Paul around 1884 and established the **Schmidt beer** brand from the landmark brewery on West Seventh Street, producing family-made beer for 130 years.

# $12$  **Saint Paul Grand Round**

This 30-mile loop is included in the venerable Saint Paul Classic bike tour in and around Saint Paul. The Classic treats riders to three main routes, with a mansion-lined boulevard to parkway pedaling, stunning river valley views, and a few respectable hills.

**Start:** Overlook at Summit Avenue and Mississippi River Boulevard

**Distance:** 30.0-mile loop in total, with many options for fewer miles

**Riding time:** 2–2.5 hours

**Best bike:** Road

**Terrain and surface type:** Flat to rolling, with a few medium-steep hills, on smooth pathways and low- to no-traffic roads

**Highlights:** Some of the best river views in the metro, easygoing riding on pathways and parkways, access to downtown Saint Paul attractions

**Hazards:** Watch traffic on parkways and road crossings.

**Map:** USGS Saint Paul West

**Getting there:** From I-94, take the Cretin-Vandalia exit and head 1 mile south to the University of Saint Thomas. Park where permitted or along Summit Avenue and overlook at the river. GPS: N44 56.496' / W93 11.881'

## The Ride

Saint Paul is a wonderfully diverse city, and the cycling scene reflects that with a spaghetti plate of bike routes wandering along wooded parkways and riverside roads from downtown to outlying neighborhoods. Take a relaxing coast along the river in the downtown harbor area, cruise winding neighborhood roads, or test your mettle on the steeps climbing

*View west from trailhead*

away from the city. This loop does all of that, following the landmark Grand Round route, synonymous with the Saint Paul Classic's mid-distance loop.

Start the loop rolling downhill from Summit Avenue's western terminus at the Mississippi River gorge, treated to great views of the densely wooded cliffs and river below. Pass under Ford Parkway and take a quick stop to look over Lock and Dam No. 1, just below the river bridge. On the other side of the road is the old Ford assembly plant, one of Henry Ford's most productive. This plant churned out Ford's first model Ts, armored cars during World War II, and ubiquitous Ford Rangers. Keep riding to the junction with MN 5. Here the route joins part of the Harbor Tour ride as it follows Shepard Road along the ridge above Crosby Farm Park to I-35E and into downtown Saint Paul. Turn left onto Eagle Parkway, past the Science Museum, for the 15-mile route of the Classic.

# Miles and Directions

**0.0** Start at Summit Avenue and Mississippi River Boulevard.

**1.7** Pass under Ford Parkway and past the former Ford assembly plant.

**3.9** Junction with MN 5; continue straight ahead and onto the bike path paralleling Shepard Road.

**6.0** Pass under I-35.

**7.7** Junction with Randolph Avenue; keep straight ahead.

**10.0** Pass through downtown Saint Paul's harbor.

**12.0** Ride across Childs Road and continue on the bike path.

**12.7** At the bike bridge, cross over Warner Road into Indian Mounds Park.

**12.9** Left turn onto the path heading uphill.

**14.3** Right turn onto Plum Street, merging onto Pacific Street.

**15.3** Left turn onto Hudson Road and a quick left onto Johnson Parkway.

**17.4** Meet the south shore of Lake Phalen. Veer left onto Wheelock Parkway.

**20.0** Junction with I-35; keep riding west.

**22.7** Arrive at the east shore of Lake Como. Hop on the bike path and turn right, following East Como Lake Drive around the top of the lake to Lexington Parkway.

**23.7** Ride across the Lexington Parkway bike/pedestrian bridge. The path will merge into Kaufman Drive. Follow Kaufman to Estabrook Drive.

**24.0** Right turn onto Estabrook Drive and a quick left onto the bike path down to Horton Avenue, where another right turn leads to Hamline Avenue.

**24.6** Left turn onto Hamline Avenue and a quick right onto Como Avenue.

**26.2** Left turn onto Raymond Avenue.

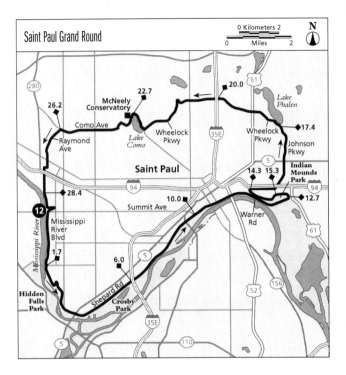

Saint Paul Grand Round

**27.5** Right turn onto Wabash Avenue.

**27.7** Left turn onto Pelham Boulevard.

**28.4** Junction with North Mississippi River Boulevard. Turn left.

**30.0** Arrive back at the Summit Avenue trailhead.

## Ride Information

### RESTAURANTS

Head to **Great Waters Brewing Company** on St. Paul's pedestrian mall for prime patio seating and a frosty mug. 426 Saint Peter St.; (651) 224-BREW (2739); greatwatersbc.com.

Since 1939, **Mickey's Dining Car** has served up thick-as-cement malts and juicy burgers, and it's on the National Register of Historic Places. 36 W. Seventh St.; (651) 698-0259; mickeysdiningcar.com.

## BIKE SHOPS

For more than thirty years, **Grand Performance** owner Dan Casebeer has shared his passion for cycling with legions of area riders, from newbies to elite pros. Active club teams, rider development, and unparalleled commitment to the sport, be it fixing a flat or sizing up your dream bike. 1938 Grand Ave.; (651) 699-2640; gpbicycles.com.

**County Cycles** started selling bikes and gear in 1981 and remains one of the state's finest. Almost-daily group rides from the shop; sponsor of the Gopher Wheelmen cycling club, founded by local rider Ken Woods in 1934. 2700 Lexington Ave. N, Roseville; (651) 482-9609; countycycles.com.

## FLORAL ARRANGEMENT

The grand glass dome and gardens inside at the **Marjorie McNeely Conservatory** were born of German inspiration in the early 1900s. George Frederick Nussbaumer, a Baden, Germany-born lad, learned the landscape gardening trade at his father's greenhouse and later worked in London's Royal Botanic Gardens. Persuaded to come to Saint Paul as a gardener by Horace Cleveland, he crafted plans for a "propagating greenhouse" at Como Park. Renamed in 2002 for Marjorie McNeely, former president of the Saint Paul Garden Club, the conservatory boasts six indoor and three outdoor gardens with more than 50,000 plants, including tropical palms and orchids, and the largest bonsai tree collection in the upper Midwest. The conservatory is a 1974 inductee to the National Register of Historic Places.

## AREA EVENTS AND ATTRACTIONS

Welcome summer at Saint Paul's annual **Grand Old Day**, 30 blocks of arts, live music, and great food on the city's favorite destination street. First Sunday in June. Free bike parking on the Ayd Mill Bridge; grandave.com/events/grand-old-day.

Don't miss live music outdoors from local bands and ensembles during **Music in the Parks** at the Como Lakeside Pavilion and the Phalen Amphitheater. Many shows are free of charge; ci.stpaul.mn.us.

The first **Minnesota State Fair** was held in 1859 near what became downtown Minneapolis. It was not until 1885, when Ramsey County donated a 210-acre parcel to the State Agricultural Society, that the fair found a permanent home at its current location; mnstatefair.org.

# 13 Gateway and Browns Creek State Trails

A perennial local favorite since its first days in 1993, the Gateway Trail takes riders from the buzz of Saint Paul's downtown area through dense wooded areas, parks, lakes, and wetlands to open meadows and rural landscapes. Ready for more? Add the new Browns Creek segment for another 6.5 fabulous miles (one way) to Stillwater's charming main street.

**Start:** Cayuga Park, 198 Cayuga St., Saint Paul
**Distance:** 18.2 miles one way
**Riding time:** 1.5-2 hours
**Best bike:** Road
**Terrain and surface type:** Primarily flat with occasional gentle hills on a smooth, two-lane paved path
**Highlights:** Brilliant variety of landscape, including densely wooded urban areas, rolling farmland, and wildlife-packed wetlands

**Hazards:** The trail intersects roads with moderate traffic flow.
**Maps:** USGS Saint Paul East; printable map available online at gatewaybrownscreektrail .org/resources/Documents/ GBCTA%20Brochure%20and%20 Map%20website%20version%20 july%2021%202018.pdf; more trail info at the Gateway Trail Association's website: gateway trailmn.org

**Getting there:** From downtown Saint Paul, follow I-35 North to the Pennsylvania Avenue exit. Turn right onto Phalen Boulevard, then make a quick left onto North Mississippi Street and another left onto East Cayuga Street. Parking is available on neighborhood roads or at Cayuga Park. GPS: N44 58.003' / W93 05.488'

# The Ride

In a leisurely 18 miles, the Gateway Trail captures the hybridization of Minnesota's urban and rural landscapes. Its humble Saint Paul trailhead is enveloped by a quiet city neighborhood just a mile northeast of the state capitol building, and only a nondescript wooden sign marks the start. Built by the Minnesota Department of Natural Resources in 1993 along an abandoned Soo Line Railroad corridor, the path is one of the most accessible and popular rail trails in the state. Traveling first through an urban residential and commercial jungle, the trail soon meets large stands of hardwood forest with dramatic views of adjoining farmland and curves through aromatic pine stands on the way into Stillwater.

Just past the din of freeway traffic, the trail passes the Gateway State Trail Community Garden and promptly recedes from the cityscape into a thickly wooded residential area. The highway behind and a verdant tunnel of trees ahead lend a blurred sense of place—are we riding in a city or a developed wilderness?

The path travels through a woodsy wonderland for roughly 4 miles and slices through the center of Phalen-Keller Regional Park, a 750-acre oasis boasting a pair of lakes, a swimming beach, fishing, paddling, and two golf courses. Spur trails branch into the park's extensive circuits for noodling around the shoreline. Beyond the park, the trail intersects the Bruce Vento Regional Trail, a 7-mile rail trail following a former Burlington Northern Railroad corridor. Named for the Saint Paul native and US representative, the Vento trail is a tempting extension to a Gateway ride. Plan a side trip south to roll through historic Swede Hollow, site of waves of 1800s-era immigrants; the Hamm's Brewery; and the city's early railroad days.

Approaching the 6-mile mark, the Gateway passes a restored wetland and returns to an urban landscape for a few miles following the Ecology Center as the trail parallels MN 36. Stop for a photo op next to the world's largest stucco snowman at the Holiday gas station—one of the trail's only convenient places for food, water, and restrooms. (I wonder how Frosty looks in Lycra?)

The ride takes on a completely new feel around mile 9, where the Gateway enters into rural Washington County. Likely to accompany cyclists and joggers on this trail segment are turtles crossing the pavement from one marshland to another (the Gateway passes an impressive fifty-eight individually protected wetland habitats) and wild turkeys rustling out from tall crops and grasses common to the area's farms. Glistening water, grazing livestock, and fields of baled hay replace views of the city. In addition to transitioning from urban to rural, the landscape also takes on characteristics of northern Minnesota, with conifers and birch trees

## THE MUNGER TRAIL

Passionate Minnesota state legislator Willard Munger worked tirelessly for environmental protection and the establishment of long-distance recreation trails. Thanks to his efforts, cyclists get to enjoy one of the longest paved trails in the United States. The Willard **Munger State Trail** runs 70 miles between Hinckley and Duluth, following the former Saint Paul and Duluth Railroad route past spectacularly scenic countryside, especially the stretch from Carlton to Duluth, where the path crosses the Saint Louis River and glides through Jay Cooke State Park.

*Aspens along the Gateway Trail*

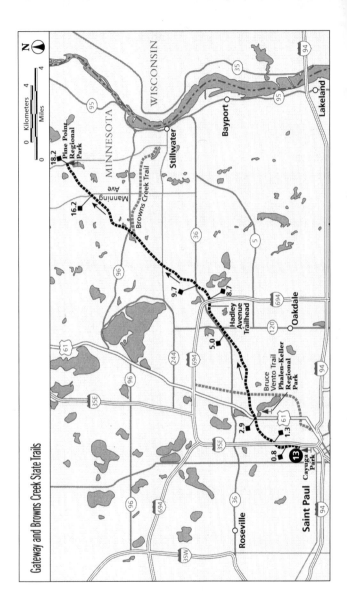

Gateway and Browns Creek State Trails

increasingly populating the trailside as the Gateway makes its way toward its northern terminus at Pine Point Regional Park, an area filled, naturally, with peaceful pines as well as restrooms, water fountains, and parking.

## Miles and Directions

**0.0** Start at the Saint Paul trailhead at Cayuga Park.

**0.8** Pass underneath Maryland Avenue.

**1.3** Cross I-35E.

**2.9** Enter Phalen-Keller Regional Park.

**4.0** Pass the Bruce Vento Regional Trail.

**5.0** Pass the giant snowman.

**7.4** Junction with Century Avenue and access to Gateway Cycle.

**8.1** Hadley Avenue trailhead, with restrooms, parking, picnic tables.

**8.7** Pass under I-694.

**9.7** Pass under MN 36.

**13.7** Cross Dellwood Road.

**16.2** Cross Historic Bridge 5721 over Manning Avenue.

**18.2** Arrive at Pine Point Regional Park trailhead. (***Option:*** The Browns Creek Trail curves along the former route of the Minnesota Zephyr tourist train for 6.5 miles from Duluth Junction through the woods into Stillwater, adding a dynamic dimension to the ride with Stillwater's stacked inventory of shops, restaurants, and riverside distractions. Also stay tuned for future mileage to the Gateway heading south to the state capitol and north to Taylor's Falls.)

# Ride Information

**RESTAURANTS**

Saint Paul's oldest family-owned Italian restaurant, **Yarusso Bros.** is a Twin Cities tradition, offering delectable home-made pasta, sandwiches, and pizza. Ride in for free pasta on the first Saturday of the month in summer. 635 Payne Ave.; (651) 776-4848; yarussos.com.

**BIKE SHOP**

Since 1992, **Gateway Cycle** has been the trailside go-to for on-the-spot repairs, gear restocking, and bike rentals. Across MN 36 at Century Avenue. 6028 MN 36, Oakdale; (651) 777-0188; gatewaycycle.com.

# 14 Big Rivers and Lilydale

This out-and-back is one of the most scenic and relaxing cruises in the metro area. The pan-flat path glides along long stretches of riverside frontage, curves around river flats forest, and scores a halfway point rest stop with postcard-worthy skyline views of downtown Saint Paul.

**Start:** Trailhead at Sibley Memorial Highway and MN 13
**Distance:** 14.2 miles out and back
**Riding time:** 1–1.5 hours
**Best bike:** Road or hybrid
**Terrain and surface type:** Flat, paved trail; short sections of road
**Highlights:** Great view of the Minnesota-Mississippi River confluence, scenic river and Saint Paul views, fun riding in wildlife-filled woods, nearby patio dining for a post-ride cooldown
**Hazards:** Use caution at road crossings, especially at the Lilydale Road railroad bridge.
**Other considerations:** Beware of water, sand, and other detritus on the trail or roads after heavy rains or spring snowmelt.
**Map:** USGS Saint Paul SW

**Getting there:** From MN 55, follow MN 12 for 0.8 mile to Sibley Memorial Highway. Make a right then a quick left into the trailhead parking and overlook. GPS: N44 51.998' / W93 10.393'

## The Ride

I remember driving along MN 13 as a kid, before I-35E was completed to the south, to get over to the Mendota Bridge and I-494. The overlook obscured by shrubbery along the road intrigued me, and today this spot offers a bird's-eye view of the treetops of the shallow Minnesota River Valley and a count-the-rivets-close vantage of jets landing at the airport.

A velvet-smooth bike path also unfurls along the river. The Big Rivers Regional Trail is one of my favorites, with its elevated views of the confluence of its namesake rivers, twisty forest sections, and stellar city panoramas.

Roll out from the trailhead and follow it across MN 13, riding along the old railbed underneath the Mendota Bridge and through the tunnel into the bluffs of Mendota, one of Minnesota's oldest original settlements. Cruise past Lucky's 13 Pub and Axel's River Grille (pick out a good spot on the patio for after the ride) and cross MN 13 again. Here the path is flanked by a limestone cliff on one side and a short way along passes the confluence of the Minnesota and Mississippi Rivers (good hiking trails over there for another day) on the way to Lilydale. When the path meets Lilydale Road, hang a left and ride past the yacht club, ditching the road in short order when the path darts into the trees. A bend in the trail at Pickerel Lake leads back across the road and into a fun stretch of curves adjacent to the river, goes under an old railroad bridge (short road section), and continues right along the riverbank. The trail briefly runs out of space where the river squeezes in and follows Water Street to the bottom side of Cherokee Park at Joy Avenue, resuming again through a corridor of dense foliage and intermittent river views to the shadow of the 160-foot Smith Avenue High Bridge. The original span was completed in 1895 and partially rebuilt nine years later after severe storm damage; it eventually deteriorated to the point of demolition. The highest in St. Paul, the landmark arched bridge links Saint Paul's Seventh Street and West Side neighborhoods. Past the bridge, a top-shelf panorama of the Saint Paul skyline emerges around a gentle bend at Plato Boulevard. This final section is a perfect place to just coast and take in the sights of Harriet Island, the

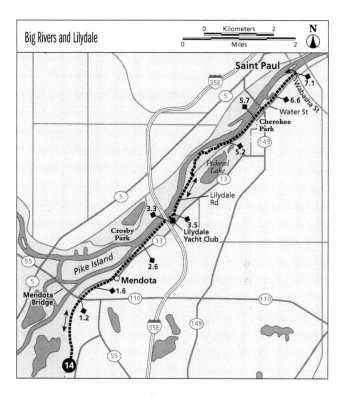

Big Rivers and Lilydale

Saint Paul

harbor, and the rarified vibe of the city's River Flats neighborhood. Hang out a bit before retracing your tracks to patio dining in Mendota and the trailhead.

## Miles and Directions

**0.0**    Start at the Sibley trailhead and overlook.

**0.4**    Cross Sibley Memorial Highway.

**1.2**    Pass under MN 55.

**1.3**    Ride through the tunnel under MN 13.

**1.6** Pass the patio dining scene behind Lucky's 13 Pub and Axel's River Grille.

**1.9** Cross MN 13 again.

**2.6** Pass the confluence of the Minnesota and Mississippi Rivers, just off your left shoulder.

**3.3** Pass under I-35.

**3.5** Turn left onto Lilydale Road. Follow the road a short distance to the continuation of the trail.

**4.3** Meet Lilydale Road again; ride straight across.

**5.2** Intersect Lilydale Road once again. Watching for traffic, ride under the railroad bridge and then back onto the trail.

**5.5** Take a short jog on the road and then back to the trail.

**5.7** Return to the trail, paralleling Water Street.

**6.2** Pass under the High Bridge.

**6.6** Junction with Plato Boulevard. Keep heading east past the Harriet Island bandshell.

**7.1** The trail "ends" under the Wabasha Street bridge. Retrace your tracks to the Sibley trailhead. (***Option:*** The riverside path continues for a bit along the river for great views of the towboats and barges.)

**14.2** Arrive back at the trailhead.

## Ride Information

### RESTAURANTS

Carbo-load in style on the backyard patio at **Axel's River Grille**, 1318 Sibley Memorial Hwy., Mendota; (651) 686-4840; axelsrestaurants.com.

Grab a burger and a cold one with friends at **Lucky's 13**, 1352 Sibley Memorial Hwy., Mendota; (651) 452-1311; luckys13pub.com.

> Lilydale's name was, not surprisingly, inspired by the water lilies that decorated nearby Pickerel Lake.

## AREA EVENTS AND ATTRACTIONS

Head to Eagan's Central Park for the summerlong **Market Fest**, with a huge farmers' market, weekly concerts, and kids art tent. Wednesday, 4 to 8 p.m. 1501 Central Pkwy.; cityofeagan.com.

# 15  Grey Cloud Island

Start this ride with a postcard-worthy Saint Paul skyline backdrop, spinning a flat warm-up before tackling a huge climb to a roller-coaster midsection through the Newport hills and long coast to the Mississippi River. This is a great mix of flats and challenging climbs, with distracting scenery, legendary pit stops, and wildlife watching.

**Start:** Battle Creek Regional Park's lower trailhead, 0.5 mile north of Lower Afton Road on Point Douglas Road
**Distance:** 14.8-mile lollipop
**Riding time:** About 75 minutes
**Best bike:** Road

**Terrain and surface type:** Mix of smooth and choppy pavement
**Highlights:** Herons, ducks, and other water-based wildlife on Grey Cloud Island; rail line and river activity near the trailhead
**Map:** USGS Inver Grove Heights

**Getting there:** From US 61, exit at Summit Avenue and turn left onto Broadway Avenue. Go 0.5 mile west to First Street and turn left onto Seventh Avenue. A left turn here leads to Levee Park. GPS: N44 84.586' / W93 00.707'

## The Ride

This short and scenic ride starts in the proud, working-class community of Saint Paul Park and tours the uber-historic Grey Cloud Island area. Pan-flat nearly the entire way, expect a leisurely cruise.

Roll out from Lion's Levee Park and ride 2 blocks over to Main Street. A right turn here takes you south through the neighborhood to CR 75 heads to a mix of open farm fields and woods. A fork in the road announces Grey Cloud

## GREY CLOUD ISLAND

Grey Cloud Island is part of the Mississippi National River and Recreation Area, a 72-mile corridor of parks, historic sites, natural areas, and a national wildlife refuge in and around the Twin Cities area. The only national park dedicated wholly to the Mississippi River, MNRRA is a "partnership park," managed by a group of like-minded businesses, regulatory agencies, nonprofits, and other landowners working to protect and preserve the Mississippi's unique natural and cultural resources. The park includes urban history of Minneapolis and Saint Paul like the old mill ruins and Stone Arch Bridge, migratory flyways for dozens of raptor species, and critical habitat for both waterfowl and terrestrial wildlife. The park's maze of coves, inlets, channels, and lakes is best explored by boat, especially the island-dotted stretch between Newport and Hastings. Farther upstream, the Minnesota Valley National Wildlife Refuge is a gold mine for birders, hikers, and solace seekers.

Grey Cloud Dunes Scientific and Natural Area, on Upper Grey Cloud Island, is punctuated by terraced sand dunes hosting a rare river-influenced prairie ecosystem with the likes of little bluestem, penstemon, and sea-beach needlegrass growing in the wind-scoured crescents and blowouts. Take a hike and look for the elusive blue racer snake slithering over the dunes.

Island Drive, veering southeast toward the river, over a short bridge, and onto the island. Even with no grand visual landmarks, there is a palpable feel of the history of this place; a subdued sense of pride of its original inhabitants pervades the island, way back to 100 BC and the time of the Woodland Mound Builders. Grey Cloud Island is also the site of the only known Native American village in Washington County, settled by a group of the Mdewakanton tribe in the 1830s.

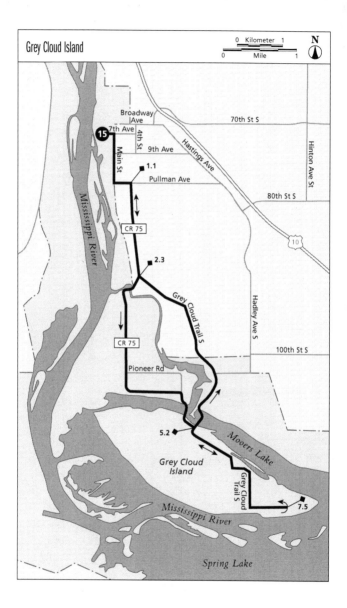

Grey Cloud Island

A flat stretch south and a hard left east brings riders to a second bridge crossing over a channel exiting Mooers Lake and around the next bend across another bridge back to the "mainland." The bridge is a great spot to stop and check out the vibrant population of waterfowl and other wildlife, including herons, ospreys, bald eagles, myriad songbirds, ducks, and geese. Curve past the Mississippi Dunes golf course and up the hill to Hadley Avenue, riding back north to Saint Paul Park and across US 61. The eastern frontage road leads through Newport, where Glen Road introduces the start of the route's closing hills. Spin a warm-up climb east on Glen Road, exiting on Woodbury Drive for nearly 2 miles of uphill to Bailey Road. Roll up and down along the ridgeline, backtracking on Sterling Avenue and finally steeply down to US 61, where a bike path parallels the highway to Point Douglas Road and the homestretch to the trailhead.

## Miles and Directions

**0.0**    Start at Levee Park; ride east to Main Street and head south.

**0.8**    Left turn onto Pullman Avenue.

**1.1**    Right turn onto Third Street (CR 75).

**2.3**    Take the right fork, following CR 75.

**5.2**    Right turn onto Grey Cloud Trail.

**7.5**    Reach the end of the point; turn around and head back from here. Ride past the CR 75 junction and continue on the Grey Cloud Trail.

**12.5**    Intersect CR 75 again. Ride north back to town, retracing your route on Pullman Avenue and Main Street.

**14.8**    Arrive back at the trailhead.

# Ride Information

## RESTAURANTS

Indulge with a half-pound burger or the Thursday-night buffet at **Tinucci's**, more than a half-century of family-owned Italian decadence. 396 21st St., Newport; (651) 459-3211; tinuccis.com.

Starting as a soda fountain sidekick of Village Drug in 1947, the **North Pole Restaurant** is still a go-to favorite for gastro delights. Roll in for a BLT and big ol' root beer float. 1644 Hastings Ave., Newport; (651) 459-9053; northpole restaurant.com.

## AREA EVENTS AND ATTRACTIONS

Mud volleyball, classic cars, and mini doughnuts at St. Paul Park's annual **Heritage Days Festival**. Third weekend in August; facebook.com/SPPHeritageDays.

# Saint Paul Mountain Biking

Fat tire trails on the Saint Paul side of the metro mix it up with a few cruiser paths and others that spend lots of time traveling the elevation profile. Head to the Mendota Trail for a woodsy river flats spin, or to Battle Creek or Afton Alps for a grueling day in the hills. Check out the scoop on the full Twin Cities mountain biking scene back on page 44.

# 16 **Mendota Trail–Eagan**

The pan-flat companion to Ride 13's lumpier affair, this 6.0-mile ride follows the Minnesota River's southern banks on a mix of single- and doubletrack on a mostly wooded heading through Fort Snelling State Park's wildlife-rich river flats.

**Start:** Trailhead parking area on MN 13 in Mendota, just east of Saint Peter's Church
**Distance:** 6.0 miles one way
**Riding time:** About 45 minutes
**Best bike:** Mountain
**Terrain and surface type:** Flat singletrack and doubletrack on hard-packed and sandy trail

**Highlights:** Close-up river views; herons, ducks, deer, raptors; Henry Sibley House
**Hazards:** Occasional downed tree limbs, sections of deep sand, waterlogged trail; watch for hikers.
**Other considerations:** Steer clear of the trail when wet to avoid damaging the route.
**Map:** USGS Saint Paul West

**Getting there:** From MN 55 at the Mendota Bridge, follow MN 110 on the south side of the river to the stoplight at MN 13. Go left and follow the curves past Saint Peter's Church to the parking lot on the left side of the road, on the hill above downtown Mendota. GPS: N44 53.241' / W93 09.907'

## The Ride

This ride starts in the shadow of Minnesota's oldest church, in one of the state's oldest towns, overlooking homesites of two of the most influential people in Minnesota's history. Longtime home of the Dakota Indians, the Mendota area also attracted the first European settlers to the young

Minnesota Territory, jump-started by a bustling fur trade headquartered in this very spot. Roll through this time warp with a warm-up spin through Mendota's 2-block main street (MN 13), and drop down the hill on D Street past the historic Sibley and Faribault houses. The stone-arch tunnel beneath the Canadian Pacific Railroad line leads to Fort Snelling State Park and the Mendota Trail. The Mississippi River is dead ahead, taking in water from the Minnesota River only a few hundred yards upstream. Ride west on wide hardpack, crossing a few intermittent mini-streams born of runoff from snow or rain, below the cement rainbow arches of the Mendota Bridge. Now paralleling the Minnesota River, a brief section of open grassland gives way to thick woods of elm, maple, and cottonwood, their dense canopy shading an impenetrable green flood of assorted shrubbery and ground-level foliage in summer. Heed not the call of nature in this section lest the plethora of stinging nettles and poison ivy leave their mark on your . . . ride. This long ribbon of the river valley has been submerged during many a wet spring, leaving dead fish hanging from tree branches and deep dunes of murky river sediment. The rising river will, of course, change the complexion of the trail, so plan accordingly; ride somewhere else when wet to keep trail damage at bay.

## MEETING OF THE WATERS

The Dakota named the confluence of the Minnesota and Mississippi Rivers *mdo-te*, or "meeting of the waters." It was a place of great spiritual and cultural significance for the Dakota and Ojibwe peoples for hundreds of years. Hike here on the Pike Island Trail from the Fort Snelling State Park Visitor Center.

Riding along the riverbank, nearly at water level, the trail passes beneath the flight path for Minneapolis–Saint Paul International Airport, and you have a good vantage for examining the underbellies of jets roaring over your head. At around the 3-mile mark, the path S-curves under the dual span of I-494 and darts arrow-straight on a boulevard-like path shadowed by an awning of giant trees. At the end of the tree tunnel, the trail morphs into singletrack and shimmies between conveniently spaced riverbank trees, with a huge expanse of wetland meadow to the south. The natural environment and wildlife habitat here share that of the Minnesota Valley National Wildlife Refuge directly across the river. One of only four urban wildlife refuges in the country, we are fortunate to have this gem so close to home. Stretching along 99 miles of the Minnesota River in fourteen linear units, the refuge provides critical habitat for more than 200 bird species and other critters, including white-tailed deer, red foxes, and snapping turtles, thriving in marshland, lakes, remnant oak savanna, and floodplain forest.

Five bridge crossings provide safe passage over river tributaries and other soggy sections, and at times the trail is simply whatever path best travels among the changing tide of sand and river debris. Don't be surprised if you're blocked altogether by high water at a few points along this stretch, but it's mostly smooth sailing during summer and fall. The trees abruptly give way to tall shrubs, then just tall grasses on the last section of wide, fast trail to the Cedar Avenue bridge.

***Notes from here:*** The bike/pedestrian bridge ramps up and parallels the buzz of the highway to the north side of the river. In the old days, you could cruise along Old Cedar Avenue and cross the equally old wood-planked bridge into Bloomington. Deemed unsafe in 2002, the span was closed

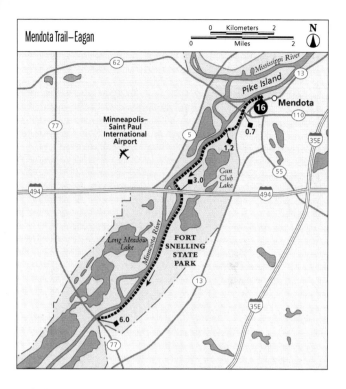

Mendota Trail–Eagan

and the planks removed, demolition imminent. However, progress is (sort of) being made between the multiple agencies involved to either renovate the existing 1920s bridge, build a new one, or come up with some other way to get across Long Meadow Lake. Meanwhile, if you are aboard a mountain bike, eyeball the skinny singletrack right on the riverbank, adjacent to the bike ramp. This little number snakes through 8-foot-tall grass and all manner of encroaching foliage to eventually join the start of the Bloomington side of the river trails—a pretty cool, Huck Finn–on-a-bike kind of adventure.

## Miles and Directions

**0.0**  Start at the Mendota trailhead on MN 13.

**0.3**  Head under the railroad tunnel into Fort Snelling State Park.

**0.7**  Pass under MN 55.

**1.2**  The trail meets and parallels the Minnesota River.

**3.0**  Pass under I-494.

**6.0**  Arrive at the junction with the Cedar Avenue trailhead.

## Ride Information

### RESTAURANTS
**Lucky's 13 Pub** in Mendota serves up good times and great food, with the Big Rivers Regional Trail right out the back door. 1352 Sibley Memorial Hwy.; (651) 452-0161; luckys 13pub.com.

### AREA EVENTS AND ATTRACTIONS
One of Minnesota's oldest cities gets its groove on in early July at **Mendota Days** with a parade, live music, and special attractions like the rolling heroics of the Twin Cities Unicycle Club. The action happens on Sibley Memorial Highway (MN 13) in Mendota. Check mendotaheights.patch.com for updated information.

# 17  Salem Hills Trails

This 4.5-mile linear trail at Harmon Park cruises a mellow course through wildflower-packed meadows and pine-hardwood forest on smooth, flowing, and gently rolling singletrack. It's the perfect place for new riders to get comfortable and gain confidence, and advanced riders can appreciate an easy trail day or speed workout.

**Start:** Harmon Park, 0.5 mile south of Upper 55th Street on Asher Avenue
**Distance:** 4.5 miles of multiple loops
**Riding time:** About 30 minutes
**Best bike:** Mountain
**Terrain and surface type:** Gently rolling on smooth, hard-packed singletrack

**Highlights:** Gorgeous scenery, low to moderate technical level and just-right distance for new riders, all on a stacked loop system; great ski trails in winter
**Hazards:** None
**Maps:** USGS Inver Grove Heights; Minnesota Off-Road Cyclists (MORC) maps available online at morcmtb.org

**Getting there:** From I-494, exit onto MN 3 (South Robert Trail) and head south 0.2 mile to Upper 55th Street. Turn left for 0.5 mile to Asher Avenue and then south to the trailhead. GPS: N44 51.925' / W93 04.403'

## The Ride

Don't let the short mileage at Salem Hills fool you. Every inch of the park's 4.5 miles is on sublime singletrack that is so addicting, plan on extra time to get your multiple-lap fix. Salem's three linked loops offer a nice mix of scenery, with a woodsy start giving way to open prairie, a small pond, and a handful of bridge crossings. This is also a regular locale for the launch of the Minnesota Mountain Bike Series, and despite the absence of a lung-busting climb or white-knuckle downhill, many racers say it's their favorite event of the year.

Start the ride heading north into the woods on the Singletrack Sawmill (other aliases being the North Loop or North Forks Trail), with just under 1 mile of snaky single-track as fine as any you'll find in the metro. Loop around and back to the south, rolling through prairie grasses and wildflowers (don't miss the blackberries in season), past the entrance trail, to the Pond Loop, introduced by a high-speed

*Singletrack snaking through the meadows*

banked corner that ejects you into rolling pine forest mixed with prairie grass. If rain has fallen within the past few days, this would be the most likely spot to encounter a puddle or two, as it is a sometimes-soggy section. A short bridge crossing past the pond leads up a little hill to the junction with the Prairie Fire (South) Loop. Sweep across gorgeous Minnesota prairie planted with native grasses and wildflowers, and be on the lookout for bluebirds frolicking about. The trail leaves the prairie and moves into a hammerhead section in the woods, then a few more prairie-to-woods-to-prairie transitions leading to the far southern part of the park. Loop back north along the fringe of the woods and back into another fun stretch of meadow to the top of the loop, then turn left into the woods for the west side of the Pond Loop, a flat cruise to one more bridge and more open country riding. Salem's one obstacle, a big ol' boulder wedged in the path, appears near the top of the loop. Conquer the rock and ride around to the final turn back to the trailhead.

*Groovy trail rep:* Salem Hills exists thanks to a team effort between MORC and the city of Inver Grove Heights when the park won a place on the International Mountain Bicycling Association's (IMBA's) Hot Spots program, a nationwide effort focusing on building singletrack in urban areas across the country.

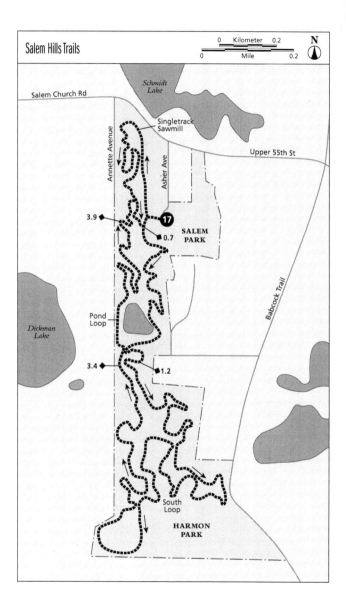

**Salem Hills Trails**

Schmidt Lake

Salem Church Rd

Singletrack Sawmill

Annette Avenue

Asher Ave

Upper 55th St

3.9 ◆

**17**

■ 0.7

**SALEM PARK**

Pond Loop

Dickman Lake

Babrock Trail

3.4 ◆

■ 1.2

South Loop

**HARMON PARK**

Kilometer
Mile

N

## Miles and Directions

**0.0**   Start at the trailhead and ride south on a clockwise loop.

**0.7**   Junction with the top end of the Pond Loop. Bear right to start the loop.

**1.0**   Ride past the pond and over a bridge.

**1.2**   Turn left to start the Prairie Fire Loop.

**3.4**   Arrive back at the top of Prairie Fire and continue on the west side of Pond Loop.

**3.9**   Junction with North Loop. Go right to finish the lap.

**4.5**   Arrive back at the trailhead.

## Ride Information

### RESTAURANTS

You can't beat a giant burrito and frosty beverage after a great trail day. Fill up at **Chipotle**, just up the road at 1857 S. Robert St., West St. Paul; (651) 552-2110; chipotle.com.

### AREA EVENTS AND ATTRACTIONS

Trade your bike for running shoes and see Salem's trails at a slower pace at the **Harmon Farms Trail Runs**, mid-September at Harmon Park (aka Salem Hills); invergrove heights.org.

# Area Clubs and Advocacy Groups

Here is a short list of the many organizations that make Minnesota a great place to ride a bike.

### Nice Ride Minnesota
Modeled after similar bike-sharing systems throughout the world, Nice Ride started with 65 bike stations in Minneapolis and has since expanded to 400, with a fleet of more than 3,000 bikes.

Users buy access to the bikes by the day, month, or year, during which time they can take one bike at a time from any of Nice Ride's locations and return it to any other location. A $75 annual subscription allows access to the bikes, with just a $2 charge for the first 30 minutes and usage fees for additional time. Get all the dirt at niceridemn.com.

### Bicycle Alliance of Minnesota
bikemn.org
Working to make Minnesota even more bicycle friendly.

### Minnesota Off-Road Cyclists (MORC)
morcmtb.org
Minnesota's mountain biking scene would not be what it is today without this dedicated group.

### Bolder Options
bolderoptions.org
Teaching and promoting healthy youth development.

**Full Cycle**
fullcyclebikeshop.org
Local shop employs and trains homeless youth.

**Open Streets Minneapolis**
openstreetsmpls.org
Advocating to make Minneapolis a better place to ride.

**Minnesota Cycling Federation**
mcf.usacycling.org
Minnesota's bike racing headquarters.

**Explore Minnesota/Pedal Minnesota**
exploreminnesota.com/pedal-mn
An invaluable route-finding tool, with area tours and events.

For more information and links to other groups, bike clubs, and teams and gear companies, check out the **Twin Cities Bicycling Club** website: biketcbc.org

# About the Author

Northland-bred scribe and self-propelled recreation junkie **Steve Johnson** grew up roaming the northern lakes and forest regions of Minnesota and Wisconsin and brings four generations of proud family heritage to this exciting book. An avid hiker and cyclist, Steve can usually be found on a hiking trail in the woods somewhere, or with his bike and a wide-open road. With a spare hour or five, he is outdoors and in tune with nature's finest.

Author of nearly twenty books and a regular contributor to *Backpacker* and other regional magazines across the country, some of Steve's other work includes two editions of *Best Bike Rides Minneapolis–St. Paul*, *Loop Hikes Colorado*, *Bicycling Wisconsin*, *Mountain Biking Minnesota*, and spinoff sporting events projects. Don't miss his new children's book, *Jack & Lauren in the Big Bog*.

Steve lives and writes in far north Wisconsin and southeastern Minnesota.